ENCOUNTERING
JESUS

Books Compiled by James Stuart Bell

FROM BETHANY HOUSE PUBLISHERS

Encountering Jesus

Heaven Touching Earth

The Spiritual World of the Hobbit

Angels, Miracles, and Heavenly Encounters

From the Library of A.W. Tozer

From the Library of Charles Spurgeon

Love Is a Flame

Love Is a Verb (with Gary Chapman)

Love Is a Verb Devotional (with Gary Chapman)

ENCOUNTERING
JESUS

Modern-Day Stories
of His Supernatural Presence
and Power

COMPILED BY
JAMES STUART BELL

BETHANY HOUSE PUBLISHERS
a division of Baker Publishing Group
Minneapolis, Minnesota

© 2015 by James Stuart Bell

Published by Bethany House Publishers
11400 Hampshire Avenue South
Bloomington, Minnesota 55438
www.bethanyhouse.com

Bethany House Publishers is a division of
Baker Publishing Group, Grand Rapids, Michigan

Printed in the United States of America

Library of Congress Cataloging-in-Publication Data
Bell, James S.
    Encountering Jesus : modern-day stories of his supernatural presence and power / compiled by James Stuart Bell.
        pages cm
    Summary: "Ordinary people who have seen Jesus, heard his voice, or experienced his miraculous intervention share their stories in this inspiring collection"— Provided by publisher.
    ISBN 978-0-7642-1279-6 (pbk. : alk. paper)
    1. Jesus Christ—Presence. I. Title.
    BT590.P75B45 2015
    232'.8—dc23   2014047385

Unless otherwise identified, Scripture references are from the Holy Bible, New International Version®. NIV®. Copyright © 1973, 1978, 1984, 2011 by Biblica, Inc.™ Used by permission of Zondervan. All rights reserved worldwide. www.zondervan.com

Scripture quotations identified AMP are from the Amplified® Bible, copyright © 1954, 1958, 1962, 1964, 1965, 1987 by The Lockman Foundation. Used by permission.

Scripture quotations identified NKJV are from the New King James Version. Copyright © 1982 by Thomas Nelson, Inc. Used by permission. All rights reserved.

Scripture quotations identified NLT are from the *Holy Bible*, New Living Translation, copyright © 1996, 2004, 2007 by Tyndale House Foundation. Used by permission of Tyndale House Publishers, Inc., Carol Stream, Illinois 60188. All rights reserved.

The following are true stories, but some details and names have been changed in order to protect privacy.

Editorial services provided by Jeanette Gardner Littleton Publication Services.

15 16 17 18 19 20 21   7 6 5 4 3 2 1

In keeping with biblical principles of creation stewardship, Baker Publishing Group advocates the responsible use of our natural resources. As a member of the Green Press Initiative, our company uses recycled paper when possible. The text paper of this book is composed in part of post-consumer waste.

To my dear daughter
Rosheen McAlister,
who encounters Jesus
on an arduous journey.

In the Son, therefore, heaven is open to the world. . . . This is the meeting place where all the roads from heaven come together at the one "gate" through which everyone who wishes to go to the Father must pass.

—Hans Urs von Balthasar

Contents

7

Contents

Acknowledgments

As always, to the professionals at Bethany House, who strive hard to make these books the best they can be. Among others behind the scenes, Andy McGuire, Ellen Chalifoux, Carissa Maki, and Erin Hollister.

Introduction

In my two most recent volumes, my compiled stories covered supernatural events of various kinds: angels, spiritual warfare, and miracles of all sorts. This volume deals with the Lord of the supernatural himself: Jesus Christ. Jesus is our all in all, He is the center point of history and of the universe, and all will culminate in Him. As we often say, "It's all about Jesus." Without Him, the Bible says, we can do nothing (John 15:5). Through Him we can do all things (Philippians 4:13). We need His grace and power to navigate life's challenges and trials.

This book seeks to reveal Jesus in new and exciting ways as He has manifested himself to these privileged individuals in circumstances that have transformed their lives. These writers at times go beyond His grace and power to a revelation of His immediate presence in their various situations. Many of these stories are one-time encounters with Jesus that have profound effects for a lifetime.

Some of the writers expressed initial reluctance to share because others may doubt their experiences. A friend of mine had an experience he felt was just too personal to share in this book. But those who have had the courage and peace to do so have richly blessed us as Jesus communicates with and even embraces them. Some of the stories are not so direct and immediate but have Him in the background guiding and intervening.

Jesus longs to reveal himself to us each day, and many of us have a greater hunger to receive His loving presence. Witness the popularity of a book like *Jesus Calling*. In one of the stories contained herein He declares, "I am your warrior." He is so many things to us, as can be seen in all His names throughout Scripture. But the main attribute that comes across in these stories is love. He is Love immeasurable, unfathomable, all-consuming. And even if you don't see Him or feel His embrace, my hope is that this collection will stir you to open your whole being to receive more and more of the love He demonstrated in His life, death, and resurrection—for you.

—James Stuart Bell

Seeing Jesus

ALEXINE CRAWFORD

I found love in Ripon Cathedral. The army had sent us to Ripon, a town in North Yorkshire, England, and in its famous cathedral we found friendliness and welcome. We started attending the parish communion service, which was a fairly new concept at that time and was held not in the big echoing nave but in the choir area. It began at 9:30, a good time for us since our two little sons—only sixteen months apart—woke early. We took turns going to the entire service.

After the sermon, one of us would push the pram with our younger son strapped inside and the older son on the pram seat or walking. In their bright red jackets they were quite noticeable—but sometimes they were noticeable instead for the noise and commotion they created. We tried to be unobtrusive in a corner of the carved choir stalls for the last hymns and communion.

We had married four years earlier. Because of the course my husband was following, we moved three times in those four years—each time into a strange house in a strange part of the country, surrounded by strangers. We were on our own, and because of the hours of my husband's study and work, I was often on my own.

I made a lot of mistakes. I became impatient with the children. I saw my short temper, my demands, my failure to love—and my need to feel loved.

As Easter approached, on Maundy Thursday the church gave an evening communion service in the cathedral. I put the children to bed in good time and left my husband in charge at home.

I was sitting on the left in the back row of the choir stalls. Two rather unprepossessing women sat in front of me, and mentally I began criticizing them. Then I caught myself and asked God to give me love.

The leader read the chapter in John's gospel about the Last Supper. And as I listened I saw an intricate vision of Jesus washing His disciples' feet. He was on His knees, his hands in the bowl of water, washing their dirt-worn feet. Great wafts of air filled me deep, deep inside.

Time came for me to go up to the altar rails to receive the bread and wine. Walking from my seat, I felt as if I were eighteen inches above the floor, floating.

My husband looked at me when I got home and asked, "What's happened to you?"

I could tell him only what I had experienced, the wonder of it, but not the full importance of it, because I did not know. All I knew was that I had seen Jesus, and that He had given me something very good.

I tried in a letter to tell my mother, and I think she felt mystified. I wrote to a dear friend who was a nun, and she replied that we should keep spiritual experiences to ourselves. So I did. I didn't try to tell anyone else about it for five long years.

We moved again, and I headed up what turned into a big Sunday school. Every Saturday evening I faced a terrible battle as I prepared a lesson and a talk for the next morning, a battle that made Saturday evenings a misery for me and an endurance test for my husband.

I did not then know anything about spiritual warfare, nor that this was a sustained enemy attack. But I prayed with my teachers each week, Sunday school went well, and the children kept coming. Two of the teachers became long-term friends, a source of much mutual blessing.

We were there for three years, and then we moved back to the area where we had started our married life, back to the evangelical church that had blessed us then and that had become vibrantly alive.

Partly there and partly through the school my kids were going to, I met a woman I did not particularly take to. But she brought something to encourage me in my Christian walk. I ended up warming up to her and telling her about what had happened in Ripon Cathedral.

She listened.

"You were filled with the Holy Spirit," she said.

Understanding and fellowship helped me to grow. But as I did grow, I realized despite my vision at Ripon, I had a problem with Jesus himself. When I listened to other people speak of Him in loving terms, I realized that I could not do that.

I remember the day when the realization hit me—I went to a friend I trusted and told her how distressed I was at this lack of knowing and understanding His love. As we prayed together, we discerned that some rejection I had received in my early life had led me to withdraw from others and reject them, probably for fear of being hurt. In turn, I was actually rejecting Jesus emotionally, rejecting His love for me, and refusing to love Him.

When I went to Him about this, I realized He forgave me.

And He also gave me fresh insight about that vision I'd had of Jesus humbling himself to carry out the menial and unpleasant job of washing His friends' feet.

I had asked for love, a simple heartfelt prayer in a church service, and Jesus showed me love so vividly that I felt I was there, actually seeing Him demonstrating His own love. As I saw Him, He poured into me the power to love.

Over the years since then, God has sent many people for me to take care of. Did Jesus choose to show himself to me in the way He did, in the hope that I would learn to serve humbly as He himself does? As I have done so, I have started to truly bask in the presence of His love.

Fifteen Seconds With Jesus

MARY JO KRUMP

A visit at night was the mother of all ironies. At night it was quiet and dark. And I was alone.

If there was an angel charged with scheduling visitations, he would have said, "Jesus, don't visit Mary Jo at night. Remember her night terrors as a kid? Remember her inherent fear of the dark? Sure, she's an accomplished professional now, an outdoor buff, and a risk taker at heart. But she harbors a secret fear of the dark. Pick another time of the day."

He didn't.

Sometimes I pass the apartment building where He came that Friday night in March of 1988 and wonder how He found it. The window to my old room is a speck on the horizon of a long stretch of buildings. Consider this tiny window from Jesus' perspective. He has an earth full of people to track and galaxies in His backyard. When I consider His omniscience, I can almost understand how I got on His radar, but here's the real puzzler: How did I get on His *schedule*?

It was the eve before a Saturday morning when I would awaken alone, without anyone to share the weekend. Going solo didn't bother me during the week when I woke up to an engaging job with a calendar full of sales meetings in the Denver area. Monday through Friday was usually followed by weekends of play in the Colorado outdoors. But not always. Not that weekend.

Sometimes that seventh morning of the week began a forty-eight-hour sweep without any significant conversation. I'm hardwired as an extrovert, so weekends alone felt as dry and desolate as a desert. I often wondered if the grocery store cashier knew that our little exchange was the only substantive conversation of my weekend. Those solitary hours reminded me that I was companionless. Like my fear of the dark, the truth about my overdose of solitude was a hidden and almost shameful core of my life.

I had reached the second half of my twenties. With a string of failed relationships that claimed portions of my heart, I relocated from the East Coast to Colorado to get a fresh start. Living at the doorstep of the gorgeous Rocky Mountains meant that some weekends were full of outdoorsy stuff with people to share the action. Like an underwater swimmer inhaling a lung-full of fresh air, I breathed in the beauty of life above ten thousand feet. I found contentment when I traversed the ski slopes, hiked a fourteener, or biked the mountain trails. The canvas of mountain activities made me forget the hefty solitude I faced when I returned home and the deeper fear that I would always be alone. I became very good at satiating my craving for company with a plateful of outdoor fun. Busyness can create a false sense of security and independence away from God.

Such was not the case that weekend. My schedule was empty. Maybe that's how I got on *His*. To awaken me as gently as Jesus did took intimate knowledge of my sleepy brain waves. I know this because I once had the opportunity to study the research of a sleep lab. I analyzed brain waves captured during sleep. They were recorded on a printout that showed patterns of sharp mountain-peak spikes and smooth, rolling hills. Those patterns revealed different stages of sleep and, among other things, indicated when it was more and less invasive to awaken someone. Now I know that in addition to the number of hairs on my head, God also knows the intricacies of my sleep patterns. He knew when to drop in.

When the sky was dark, my most vulnerable time, Jesus came. I have never experienced psychosis or any mental break from reality, nor did I that night. I was completely lucid, fully alert, and of sound mind.

I was lying on my back when I felt my eyes open. At the same time, my head rolled to the right toward my window. That's when I saw Him. Sleep-induced cobwebs didn't veil my sight. There wasn't any rush of adrenaline that caused me to scream in alarm, "Someone is in this room, and it's freaking me out!" With my longstanding fear of the dark and the fact that I was alone, this is the response I would have expected. I would look back at this moment and marvel at the fullness of the truth in 1 John 4:18: "Perfect love drives out fear." Perfect Love entered my room that night and cast out all fear. There's simply no other explanation. There was no other way I would have awoken to an unexpected visitor and not have been completely terrified.

The instant I opened my eyes, they found their spot. At once I recognized the face of the man. Jesus. I knew Him as surely as I would have known the face of my own earthly father. The face I saw was identical to the one on the cover of my Jesus book from childhood. It was instantaneously familiar, as if I had traveled back in time to the spot where I used to sit cross-legged on the floor and hold that book in my seven-year-old hands. The kindness in the eyes of the man on the book cover and in the eyes of the man who stood by my bed was the same. His soft compassion contradicted the scary "fire and brimstone" messages I heard about God at my childhood church and my private elementary school. Mary Jo the little girl used to cringe at the horrifying warnings. My religious teachers categorized the pile of sins that had the power to launch me straight into hell. The teachings instilled a deep-seated stronghold of fear that took root in my life as early as five years old. As soon as I left for college, I ditched the religious rules and rigid stipulations and felt the great relief of freedom.

But God knew how to get my attention. He remembered the image that compelled me to see the real Jesus. I don't know where my Jesus book is now, but I'll never forget that face. I knew who stood by my bed.

The curtains in front of my window provided a backdrop for Jesus' form, which was suspended a little above bed level. He looked at my body, not directly into my eyes. He held His hands a little above hip level with palms facing upward. His eyes looked upon my body and then up through the ceiling, up toward His Father. Twice He glanced from my body to the Father, two times perhaps to match the two-part unspoken message, which was as clear as a bell and gentle as a caress: "I'm interceding to the Father for you, and I'm going to take care of you."

And those eyes! They were windows to a sea of love, and their blue sparkle was more divine than human. The depth of their compassion was ineffable—beyond words. Are Jesus' eyes really blue? I don't know, but those were the color of the eyes that came alive, right off the cover of my childhood book; they were the eyes that spoke to me that night.

He didn't say good-bye. It ended. He was gone, but it didn't feel abrupt.

Fully composed, I leaned onto my right elbow and reached with my left hand to turn on the light by my bed. I wasn't shaken, and to this day, over twenty years later, I remember my calm nonchalance as I slunk back under the bedcovers. I didn't sit up, make a phone call, check the door locks, or search my apartment. Instead, I laid my head back onto my pillow, and sleep greeted me like a warm blanket.

The next morning I awoke and felt a peace unmatched before or since. The dreaded Saturday morning blues never came.

I haven't written about my vision until now. I did not understand why Jesus came to see me, nor the importance of sharing my story. When it happened, I was a new Christian and didn't appreciate the enormousness of His visit. Even now, after time has passed and my knowledge of Jesus has grown, I still hesitate to write this account because there will surely be those who won't believe me, and worse, there will be some who think I'm elevating my relationship with Jesus above theirs. The truth is, I'm a self-proclaimed work in progress and have much more to learn. But I've decided that if Jesus could take the time to visit me—a newbie Christian who would take years to understand the fullness of His message—then I can tell my story without further ado.

Why *did* Jesus come to see me?

I think He showed up by my tiny apartment window to set the record straight. The scary childhood messages that made me feel like God was more annoyed with me than in love with me just weren't true.

Jesus also gave me a front-row view of His character. Instead of staying in the safe and easy periphery of my life, Jesus stepped right into the battle zone. He came to me at night when I should have been terrified; He came to show me that my fears cannot coexist with His love. He gave me a glimpse of the Perfect Love, the only love with the power to cast out fear. He proved the vigor of His love by coming at the precise time of the night when I was most vulnerable. Then He left me with a gift of unimaginable, perfect, and profound peace that I will someday know for all eternity.

Why would Jesus show up for any of us at all—vision or no vision? It doesn't take an experience like mine for Jesus to intimately enter our lives, and we all can have a front-row view of His character. It's the humbling of His supernatural, superhuman self that makes His presence in our most ordinary, human lives all the more extraordinary. It's His attention to the detail in our lives that makes the magnitude of His love so mind-boggling.

Whenever I drive past my old apartment building and the window that somehow got on Jesus' radar, I think of how we all have windows to our lives. They may seem insignificant against the canvas of the universe, but God has keen eyes for them. The booming expanse of our world, our galaxy, our universe, and beyond is never too large to prevent God from putting the spotlight on you. Jesus knows the intricacies of your life, and the Bible says He is doing the same thing for you that He reminded me of that night long ago. He is interceding to the Father for you, and He longs for us all to know His love that casts out fear.

Secure in His Embrace

JEAN ANN WILLIAMS

My twenty-five-year-old son, Joshua, died by suicide in our home on the morning of March 16, 2004.

At some point in those first few hours after the accident, a tall, thin young man stood before me. He wore a kind expression as he told me he was the city detective. He knelt on one knee, eye level with me where I sat on the sofa. "Mrs. Williams, were you in the house when your son shot himself?"

Stunned from the death of my youngest child, I could not even form words. Fear overwhelmed me as I thought about my son never breathing again.

As I quivered on the couch, Jesus' name thumped a rhythm inside my head. I stared at the detective and said, "Jesus, Jesus, Jesus."

His look held mine, and his eyes got shiny. "I'd better talk to you later, Mrs. Williams."

He got off his knee and gave me a bit more time to pull myself together.

From the moment I held my dying son and felt his last heartbeat, the shock and sorrow registered high on my Richter scale. My spirit, as though it had been in a quake, was swallowed whole by the sorrow of the world.

During the days after my experience repeating Jesus' name, I would run to Him at any given moment. In the weeks that followed, grief, guilt, and a longing for my son took over my existence. As the months cumulated, I feared I'd go insane living in the house where Joshua died.

The Lord had other plans.

If God spoke our language, I'd expect Him to say to me when I reach heaven, "Sister in Jesus, you were a hard nut to crack."

My upbringing had required me to possess a certain amount of inner strength. I was born the eldest of a large family, and my childhood was cut short at age ten when my mother became disabled. I bossed my siblings, ran our home, and grew tough. To add to the difficulties, Mom's emotional distance from us children became the first important loss of my life.

I've often wondered if God allowed the sorrow of losing a maternal attachment to prepare me for the loss of my son decades later. Then I would think, *Why the heavy losses in my life?*

God had a plan for me; I just didn't know how it would unfold.

The third year of living in the same house after Joshua's death, I continued to cling to Jesus spiritually. However, the Lord kept silent as my questions mounted.

Why didn't we understand Joshua was capable of suicide? Where were the signs? Would you help me fit the puzzle pieces together, Lord? You know the why of Joshua's death.

Instead of answers from Jesus, condemning words of Satan tortured me as he stoked the fires of parental failure. *I must not have loved him enough since he chose to take his life. What did I do wrong? Where did I go wrong?*

There is no turning back to make it right. No second chances when a child takes his own life.

At this stage of grief, I didn't blame God, nor did I feel anger toward Him. You can be sure my questions turned into demands, though.

Stripped of all niceties, I knelt before Him and said, "Lord, you hear my thoughts, ugly and all. I'm telling you, I hate what you've allowed. I would be a liar if I said I'm okay with losing Joshua. I'm not."

After my rant, I didn't understand why God didn't order bolts of lightning to strike me dead. Maybe that's what I hoped for, since I had become so tired of the struggles of life without Joshua.

Another time, underneath the spray of a morning shower, I screamed to Jesus, "I've held on to you every day since Joshua's death, yet I sense a wall between us. And you know what, Lord? I'll *never* let you go. You can be silent for the rest of my life, but I won't stop needing you. Do you hear me?"

Spent from my anger, I sensed a communion with Jesus. Was this what He had wanted all along? I didn't dare be that honest with Him before, for I was taught never to become angry before the Lord.

Still, the weary, long days without Joshua stretched me. And an old friend said it best: "Those who have suffered traumatic loss have one foot on earth and one foot in a spiritual place with Jesus. We are changed."

As year four approached, I realized I had worked overtime to maintain some strength for my loved ones. They, too, missed

Joshua the son, brother, friend, grandson, and nephew. Now, being intensely weary, I found the smallest tasks a challenge. The latter parts of my days were by far the worst; the tears flowed like a waterfall at night.

One evening I decided life was not worth the effort. I begged God to stop my beating heart. I went to my husband and said, "I want to be with my Joshua."

My husband helped me to our bed, tucked the quilts around me, and stood guard as I wept. I didn't cry myself to sleep, though. My tears gushed for hours, while I tossed in torment.

I don't want to do this anymore, Lord. I'm done. Really, really done. Why did you allow me and my family to lose Joshua? I'm lonely without him. How will I go on without my child? How will my husband? What about Joshua's two siblings?

As my tears slowed, I whispered to the Lord, "I know sorrow comes to all people. I'll work at trusting you better, God. Please show me how."

During the pre-dawn hour, I finished the work of surrendering my capable self over to Jesus. I closed my swollen eyes, feeling like a shell of who I once was. Imagine your body and mind empty. Empty of energy. Empty of your own agenda. The soul becomes ready to accept whatever God plans for your life.

In other words, I came to a place where I knew I was heavenly spent. That was not the end, though, but a new beginning.

For the next few weeks I walked in a state of disconnect. I appeared, even to myself, as a walking crybaby, wanting nothing more than to be left alone. My family saw the situation as dismal. I, on the other hand, wondered if what took place as I cried that night caused an important spiritual shift. I didn't pretend to understand, but I wondered if I would forever be a solemn person.

I was lying in my room alone one evening under the warmth of my blankets. I needed a miracle.

"Jesus, I wish you could wrap your arms around me and make me feel safe," I whispered.

Moments passed and a sensation came, as if someone had added another blanket to my top quilt. I leaned on an elbow and stared across the room. My husband was nowhere around, and no extra quilt had been placed over me. I swallowed in uneasiness, lying back on my pillow. Was my mind playing tricks?

I didn't understand the comforting pressure that covered the length of my body. Then I remembered my request and whispered, "Are you here, Jesus?"

The weight around my shoulders intensified like a hug. I smiled in the darkened room, with glad tears in my eyes.

Now I understood.

The hour after Joshua died, I heard the name of Jesus filling my spiritual being. I spoke the name *Jesus, Jesus, Jesus*, as a response to the detective's question. At that moment on the morning of March 16, 2004, Jesus showed me He would love me even though my son took his own life.

Being who He is, Jesus crawled into the pit of death with me. Then, coming full circle, He embraced me as He helped me climb back out into the dawn of a new beginning.

During the days following Jesus' embrace, I had no desire to analyze what happened. The wall between God and me fell away the moment of Jesus' embrace. Now I realized God had heard my every question, saw each tear I cried, and held me when I trembled so badly I didn't even know He was holding me.

After Jesus' embrace, our house sold and we moved. The relief of leaving the house where Joshua died and moving on to the new adventure of retirement made me grateful.

I'm tougher now, in a God way, but at times I block His power by being independent. That makes me a weakling once again. There are times God reminds me I'm feeble so I won't forget that my new strength is not driven by my power. With this understanding and His grace I continue to walk uphill the grief path of suicide loss.

Now I share my experiences with other mothers. I tell them how God has shown me mercy through the love of His Son. I've stretched one foot toward heaven and, as I help them, I keep the other planted firmly on earth.

The Angel of the Lord

GUADALUPE C. CASILLAS

That's odd, I thought after I put my son to bed one night. As he slept, I heard his labored breathing. He didn't have a cold, allergies, or asthma. He had been fine all day and during our bedtime story ritual.

Before ten-year-old Ed fell asleep, he had listened to me read him a story from his children's Bible. This nightly routine was a special time for me to tuck in my son and tell him about God.

After I read, I turned out the light and snuggled next to my son. We talked until he fell asleep—a precious way to end the day.

But as he fell asleep, I heard an unfamiliar sound. His breathing was different.

Is he suddenly sick? I wondered. My overprotective motherly instincts stirred. *He sounds terrible. Will he stop breathing during the night and die?*

I considered spending the entire night next to him to monitor his breathing.

Should I wake him up and take him to the emergency room? I stayed a few more minutes to see if his condition would improve, but it didn't change. Was I overreacting?

As Ed slept, I knelt by his bedside and prayed, "Lord, I don't know what's going on with Ed, but I know you'll take care of him even if I don't stay next to him. I'll trust you and go to my bed. Please give me the assurance and peace to know that even when I'm not next to Ed, you'll be with him. Please protect him during the night and don't let anything bad happen to him. In Jesus' name, I pray."

I left my son's room to climb into my bed with my husband. Confident that God would take care of Ed, I felt God's peace and fell asleep right away.

The next morning, my younger son, Andrew, rushed downstairs to eat his cereal before school. Ed followed him and seemed to be fine.

"Brush your teeth and get dressed. Come on, we don't want to be late to school," I told the boys.

After the boys went to school, I cleaned the house and ran errands. The hours flew and it was soon time to pick up the boys. When they climbed into the car, the usual conversation started.

"How was your day?"

"Good."

"What did you learn? Are you hungry?"

Then Ed announced, "Mom, I saw an angel last night."

"You mean you dreamed about an angel?"

"No, Mom. I saw one."

"What do you mean?"

My son told me that he had awakened in the middle of the night struggling to breathe.

"Go on. . . ."

"Mom, I was scared. I couldn't breathe. All of a sudden, I saw a bright light in my room. Then I saw the angel and he told me, 'Do not be afraid, for the Lord is with you.'"

"What did he look like, Ed?"

"He had a long white robe."

"Did you see his face?"

"No. The light was too bright."

"You said he talked to you. What did his voice sound like?"

"Soothing. Like running water. Oh, Mom, he said he was the angel of the Lord. He had a golden sash around his waist."

The Angel of the Lord? Could it be? The Bible refers to Jesus as the Angel of the Lord. Was Jesus the One who came to Ed's rescue?

Now my breathing accelerated and my eyes grew wide.

"What happened next?" I asked.

"I was not afraid, Mom. My breathing was normal and I went back to sleep."

"Ed, last night after you fell asleep you were breathing kind of strange. I didn't know whether I should stay with you the whole night or not. I prayed for God to protect you even if I wasn't there to watch over you."

My fears had been real after all. My son's breathing had actually become worse and he had struggled for air. Amazed by God's love and protection, I asked Ed, "Did you know that when the Bible speaks of the 'Angel of the Lord,' it's referring to Jesus?"

His eyes locked into mine.

"Ed, I believe it was Jesus who came to help you."

My son was elated and thrilled to tell his dad and my family about it later.

I thanked God for watching over Ed. That tangible moment has kept the heart of an overprotective mother at peace through all these years. God will always be with my son—wherever he is.

Ed is now thirty years old. One afternoon as we went to lunch, he was overwhelmed with concerns about his future. I reminded him about his childhood encounter with Jesus when he struggled to breathe, and told him that Jesus would also lead him by the hand to face the challenges of this life.

"Mom, so many years have gone by. I've wondered if it was only a dream."

"I know it wasn't a dream, Ed. You know how I know this? Your abnormal breathing worried me and I asked God to protect you. Plus, how could you—at ten years of age—know Jesus has a golden sash around His waist? I didn't know that either. Months later, after you told me about your encounter, I came across a passage in the book of Revelation, chapter one, that said, 'Someone like a son of man, dressed in a robe reaching down to his feet and with a golden sash around his chest' (v. 13). So I looked up the word *sash* and found another verse in Isaiah 11 referring to Jesus: 'Righteousness will be his belt and faithfulness the sash around his waist'" (v. 5).

My son realized it had not been a dream. Jesus had heard the prayer of a mother who knew that even though she wasn't physically with her son, God would be there.

I know God watches over my sons. He ordained their days before one of them came to be. And He still keeps watch at night over them, and my grandchildren as well, as they sleep.

The Master Carpenter

Susan M. Watkins

A miracle awaited us in a dark corner of my great aunt's garage.

Originally it had been a heartfelt gift, but then it was removed from the warmth of the recipients' home and placed in an abandoned corner.

Sixty years passed. We saw my great aunt at a family reunion at the same time that my family became impassioned Christians. Seeing our transformation, my great aunt remembered her former gift and went to collect the forsaken item.

Pulling the chain on the single light bulb suspended by a wire, Aunt Marie shuffled to the corner and removed the faded oilcloth. Hesitant when staring at the darkened scar on the carving, she resolved to give it a new home.

She approached Mom with her forlorn offering. I watched from the sofa as Aunt Marie turned around the large piece of wood. Her brother-in-law, Joseph, well known for his exemplary carpentry skills, had designed and executed this personal project. A hand-carved image of *The Christ* peeked out through layers of dust at its new owner.

The carving was beautiful. A bearded Christ gazed slightly toward heaven with only His robe stained red. A wide, intricate oak leaf border surrounded the figure; the rest was stained in varied shades of brown. It also bore the artist's signature and was dated 1914.

Aunt Marie and Mom wept as the family heirloom changed hands, underscored with Mom's oath to care for it like a museum curator.

Aunt Marie's voice softened as she reminisced about this gift her brother-in-law had carved with love for her and her late husband. Her tone lowered as she spoke of the accident that had disfigured it. A heavy gear-shaped object had slashed across Christ's face—chewing an arc-shaped pattern symmetrically from top to bottom before removing a piece of the raised wooden edge. It was an unforgiving assault, an inch wide and ten inches long.

The wood was deeply imprinted by the weight of the object that left a black stain in its path. Upon closer inspection, the exposed wood had deeply yellowed from age. What was formed by talented love had become deformed by the unforeseen.

My aunt repeatedly apologized for its damaged condition, but that further engaged Mom's appreciation. She embraced Aunt Marie in gratitude and assured her that she still saw the Lord's beauty in the treasured gift, which was soon prominently displayed in our living room. Whenever my aunt visited, she was so pleased to see our care of her former possession.

Our newfound faith positioned Christ centrally in our home. As Mom learned more about the Lord and His longing to answer our prayers, she began to reflect. We sat in our living room and often discussed our sixty-year-old heirloom. The disfiguring scar bothered Mom the most. It was hideous, but we seemed to have no choice but to accept the damage, for it was a deep wound darkening with age. However, the *D* in our family's DNA stands for *Determined*, and Mom decided to launch a restoration quest.

She started her journey with the figure wrapped in soft towels and tucked into an innocuous shopping bag. An acquaintance in wood restoration expressed interest in seeing the piece. After careful examination, he exhaled and broke the bad news: It was irreparable, and attempting restoration would damage it further.

Mom was momentarily disappointed, but the first expert had recommended another. Mom rode public transportation across Chicago with her prized possession. Turning off his lighted magnifier, the second craftsman looked over his eyeglasses and confirmed that it was not fixable. It would cause more damage trying to correct the accident. With her treasure wrapped again in protective towels, Mom returned home.

I'd heard Mom's prayers as she asked for guidance to remove the immovable. She learned of a man who restored antique wooden pianos. But holding Christ's likeness in his hands, he shook his head. The damage was too deep and too old. Even heat wouldn't lift the compressed wood. Offering the same hopeless news a third time, he asked if she'd met with anyone at the Art Institute of Chicago. If it could be repaired, they could do it.

Mom made the long trek into the heart of our city. Ascending the stone steps guarded by lions, she was escorted into the core of the historic museum for her appointment in the Department of Conservation.

The master conservator complimented the artist's workmanship before he studied the deep blemish. Silently standing behind his magnifying visor and under bright lights, he evaluated the face of Christ. Years of restorative expertise at the senior level punctuated his every word. It was irreparable. The attempted restoration by their team of experts would cause more damage and discoloration to the already marred area. He suggested she focus on the remaining beauty and ignore the flaw.

Shrouded in towels a final time and transported home on buses, subways, and trains, the figure was returned to its wall and Mom told us about this fourth confirming opinion.

Some people say health cannot be fully appreciated without sickness, joy without sorrow, prosperity without poverty. For a brief while the wooden Christ wasn't discussed, but I knew my mother well enough to know she wasn't finished. Her silence meant one thing—she was praying for direction.

As a new believer, I wondered if Jesus had interest in inanimate objects. People, yes. Animals, certainly. The Bible is full of their recorded histories. Plants and trees? The fig tree and Jonah's vine withered at His word. Insects? Ask Egypt's pharaoh. Water? Stood at attention or laid flat on command.

But wood? The damaged wood of a treasured family possession? It seemed beyond the boundary, too insignificant to capture the Almighty's attention.

Soon after that, Mom announced the final phase in her restoration plan. I braced myself. She was going to appeal to a final Carpenter. Born in Bethlehem and raised in Nazareth. No stranger to a work apron filled with iron nails. Learning His dad's trade, He probably repaired Mary's table or chair, and even the neighbors' broken items.

This Carpenter was familiar with wood and nails. Mom told Him the damage detracted from His beauty, calling attention to the flaw instead of Him. She asked the Master Carpenter to restore the carving's original splendor.

All experts confirmed it could not be repaired—a man's hand was unable to reverse the situation. Mom actually prayed for a miracle regarding a piece of wood.

Time passed and nothing changed. Mom handed her problem to God, persistently reminded Him, and waited for His solution. She believed water came from rocks; coins appeared in fishes' mouths; thousands were satiated with a child's lunch; hungry lions refused to eat; and hot furnaces failed to burn flammable bodies. Mud mixed with holy spittle banished blindness; stars became calculators to tally a new nation; donkeys spoke to the rebellious; and ears were reattached in gardens. Whales carried undigested prophets to God's destinations; blown horns could topple massive walls; and garden tombs opened with a word.

Sterling history from a pristine Savior made belief possible.

Months later, while I watched television in our living room and the carved portrait hung silently behind me, Mom walked in to speak with me. As she left the room, she saw Christ's portrayal askew and promptly straightened it.

Again, she popped into the room for further discussion. We chatted and, exiting a second time, she noticed the picture was off-center. Without thinking, she again straightened it.

Another mental point ushered her back in to tell me one last thought. Finishing, she turned to leave and discovered the picture required adjusting a third time.

Wondering now if I was teasing her, she asked if I moved the picture.

Turning from the television, I glanced at her to deny involvement, when something caught my attention. Mom was talking over her shoulder while she straightened her Beloved's likeness.

I slowly rose to my feet, trying to get her attention. Then I shouted, "Mom, look! Look at the picture! It's gone!"

I reached her just as she visually followed my pointed finger and saw my view. We hugged, jumping up and down, with shouts and tears of gratitude. Attempting composure, we ran our trembling fingers over perfected wood.

Ten inches of double black rows of chewed, flattened wood were *completely* gone—utterly smooth and without a trace of the former damage. No visible repair, just seamless wood in the same color and structure of the surrounding sixty-year-old wood. Flawless restoration. Had we not seen its former condition, it would be impossible to detect the Master Carpenter's touch. Our family heirloom was completely restored to its original beauty.

Mom lifted it off its nail, brought it to the kitchen table, and with magnifying glass in hand, she studied it under our fluorescent lights.

As she completed her inspection and shed grateful tears, I left the two of them alone. In that holy moment, I collapsed onto the sofa and tried to logically figure out what had happened.

It wasn't about the wooden portrait of Jesus. It never was. That afternoon He pulled back a celestial curtain and let Mom and me take a long look at Him. In an ordinary moment on an ordinary day, He visited our home. And He did this so quietly that it took three times of moving His handiwork before we discovered His answer to our sincere request.

The news spread quickly. Many family and friends came to see what the Lord had done. Clergymen, laymen, the curious, and cynics; however, none was more amazed than my sweet Aunt Marie. She wept while running her fingers over the miraculous restoration.

There was no shrine or velvet ropes, but this has remained a powerful tool to bring glory to Christ. People were most amazed that the Lord actually took the time to restore something so insignificant. They left with personal epiphanies of His intricate concern for their lives. For if He cared enough to answer the prayers of a determined woman over a mere wooden carved portrait, they understood that surely their bigger concerns mattered to Him.

I have now walked with Christ thirty-nine years. Looking back, this experience was but a dot on my spiritual landscape, for I have beheld His power in far mightier ways. Yet this unconventional miracle taught me things I needed for the road ahead.

Just as the sun rises and sets, the stars twinkle, and snow caps mountains, so does my portrait silently declare God's uninterrupted presence in our everyday lives. It underscores His willingness to deliver our answer, no matter how trivial it may seem. Our concerns are His priority, and His approval blankets our lives.

My one-hundred-year-old suspended miracle graces my wall to this day. I treasure its significance and the two carpenters' expertise that fashioned it. Mom's tenacity, coupled with her belief in the Lord's endless abilities, stands as an unchallenged testament of His faithfulness to His children. It is profoundly true that nothing is unimportant to God when it reaches His ears in earnest. What matters to us, matters to Him.

Jesus Prays for Papa

CONNIE A. BECKMAN

When my only brother suddenly died of a massive heart attack at the age of fifty-seven, I was devastated. My brother had been my best friend while we were growing up. We were both extremely shy and withdrawn as children, and we depended on each other for companionship and reassurance.

Even though Jack had been my best friend when we were kids, he was still my big brother who occasionally liked to tease me—especially when Mom and Dad were not around.

One time Jack dug out our baby books. As we looked through them he pointed out that the book chronicling his early years was full of writing and baby pictures. He also pointed out that my baby book had a lot of blank pages and few pictures.

"I think you were adopted," he concluded.

As a little girl I didn't know what the word *adopted* meant, but I thought it must be something horrible or weird.

Later I asked Mom if I was adopted. She was surprised at my question. Mom showed me my birth certificate and told me about the day I was born. I knew for certain that I was not adopted, and I promptly informed my big brother of this.

Jack liked to tease me, but if someone else was picking on me, Jack came to my defense. And when kids in our neighborhood picked on him, I came to my brother's aid. We had each other's backs.

As an adult, Jack was my strong, steady, reassuring rock to lean on when life dealt me a curve ball or two. When I was having marriage difficulties I'd call him on the phone, and he had an amazing gift of being able to calm me down. When I faced what seemed to be overwhelming mountains of problems, Jack always managed to help me break them down into manageable molehills. He was my encourager and my protector.

Even though we lived two states apart, we were only a phone call away. We would spend hours on the phone reminiscing about childhood memories and sharing our joys and sorrows with each other.

Jack was a loving husband to his beautiful wife, Diana; a dedicated father to three grown children, Brian, Tony, and Tammy; and a fantastic grandpa.

His joy came from being around his grandchildren. Jack became like a child with them, and I always thought of Matthew 19:14, where Jesus said, "Let the children come to me. Don't stop them! For the Kingdom of Heaven belongs to those who are like these children" (NLT). He was "Papa" not only to his own children but also to his friends'.

Jack couldn't quote a lot of Scripture or talk about the deep truths of theology, but he walked with a simple faith and a humble love. For a couple of years, Jack really wanted to have another grandson, so he asked God if it was His will to bless him with a grandson. He was delighted to learn his son Brian and his wife, Mary, were expecting a baby. When the ultrasound showed a boy, Jack knew his simple prayer had been answered. He was so excited about God answering his prayer.

Jack got to hold his grandson, little Jack, minutes after he was born.

The night Jack had his massive heart attack, Diana called Brian and Mary in California. Brian and Mary began to pray. Little Chloe, their four-year-old, was also praying in her room for Papa Jack. She came running out and exclaimed: "Daddy, Daddy, I saw Jesus in the clouds praying for Papa."

Then she returned to her room and ran back out again and said, "Daddy, I saw the angels taking Papa to heaven."

I believe that Papa Jack was granted one more little miracle before he left this world to enter his heavenly reward. Jesus allowed little Chloe to see Him in the clouds praying for her Papa Jack. And she saw her grandpa being carried into heaven by the angels. Chloe's childlike faith and vision of Jesus gave the family much needed peace and hope during this sad and difficult time. And it will bolster our faith for as long as we live.

Seeing Him More Clearly

GENI J. WHITE

Where's that spectacular beauty of Oregon I've heard about?" I asked my brother the day I flew in from Illinois to his home in Coos County, Oregon. Fred, who worked for the Bureau of Land Management as a pine tree geneticist, said he and Mom, who lived nearby, would show me Oregon's best.

The next morning my brother drove Mom, my young Weimaraner hunting dog, Turk, and me up a coast range mountain and across a place called Scare Ridge. Scary indeed. The steep, tree-covered hillsides dropped a thousand feet on both sides of the narrow forest road. Gripping the seat back ahead of me, I prayed for calmness and safety. In spite of my anxiety, I enjoyed the amazing beauty.

"Wanna swim?" Fred asked as he halted his Jeep on an open plateau.

"Sure. Where?"

My brother showed me a dam across a treeless mountain ravine that meandered downward from the plateau. The pool behind the dam existed for helicopter pilots who would lower huge buckets, load them with water, and dump them on forest fires.

Fred scurried off a half mile to climb Douglas fir trees, checking tree pollens. The water lured me with the thought of refreshing exercise after my long plane trip west.

Fred hadn't mentioned that this twenty-foot-deep pond was lined with shiny black plastic to prevent water from seeping into the ground, nor that the plastic was covered in slippery brown silt.

Mom, shocked that I'd skinny-dip, agreed to watch my clothes while I enjoyed the water. Seventy-pound Turk was trained to retrieve birds from lakes and ponds but had never gone swimming. This pond presented a great chance to give him some experience. Dogs can innately swim. But Turk didn't know that.

Uncertain about entering the pool since I don't like swimming in cold water, I bent the bows of my new black steel-framed glasses—tightening them so they couldn't fall from my face—and stepped to the edge of the pond.

I skidded on the silt-covered plastic and splashed in the water. It felt as good as I'd expected.

Stroking to the middle of the pool, I called Turk. He slid on the plastic, dunked underwater, and surfaced. Panting fast, tongue out, breathing heavily, his fear-widened yellow eyes focused on me, his haven of safety. He paddled furiously.

I'm not a strong swimmer and realized that if he tried to climb on me, he would push me under.

"Help, Lord," I yelled, panicked.

At that instant, I felt something like invisible hands lift my black-rimmed glasses from my ears and nose. I watched the frames arc upward a couple of feet and drop toward the water between me and the quickly approaching dog.

No tree branches were within a hundred yards to knock those glasses off my head and into the water. No breeze swept across the quiet pond to bump them into the silt-brown water. Nothing ordinary lifted my glasses upward and off my face before letting them fall into the pool. Something—or Someone—had gently lifted those frames.

But at that moment, I didn't think about the strangeness. Time only for a lightning decision. "Do I rescue my glasses? Or escape drowning because of my dog?"

The black frames sank into the water just beyond my outstretched arm.

I desperately speed-stroked for the opposite shore. Turk scratched my back with his claws, trying to climb on me, but I spurted ahead and finally crawled from the pond.

The dog reached shore, shook moisture from his coat, and wagged his tail, as if happy about his watery adventure.

When Fred returned, he announced that my glasses were forever buried in the depths, the pond too deep and water too murky to locate them. What a bummer! I was legally blind without those lenses.

That ended my anticipation of seeing Oregon's natural beauty. Too broke to buy new glasses for a couple of weeks, I swallowed tears of frustration.

I'd longed to see without glasses ever since my teenage years, when I'd first been declared legally blind unless I wore thick lenses.

Wait! Instead of buying new glasses, I had a perfect opportunity to pray for healing. Mom and my sister-in-law prayed with me. Nothing happened after we prayed, and for a week, I viewed Oregon as colorful but fuzzy, a huge disappointment.

When my visit was over, Mom handed me to a flight attendant at the Portland airport, who settled me into my seat on the plane. My husband rescued me as I disembarked at O'Hare in Chicago.

The following Sunday after church, I sensed a strong urge to ask our pastor for prayer. As he leaned on the pulpit and prayed for healing of my eyes, we strongly sensed God's presence. He quoted the verse, "If we know that he hears us . . . we know that we have what we asked of him" (1 John 5:15).

The Spirit, so powerfully present, left no doubt—our prayer was heard. With awe, our pastor said, "Walk in faith." I promised I'd tell him when God answered.

At home the next six weeks, I swept floors by measuring whether I'd moved the bristles six inches ahead of previous broom strokes. So frustrating. My husband, Bob, had to leave work early to buy groceries, a hassle for him. I slurped meals with my face six inches from my plate to fork up meat or veggies or salad. An embarrassment.

Late one dark October night, Turk nudged me with his nose. I was too drowsy to think about how unusual it was for Turk to wake me in the night.

Years earlier I'd learned to navigate in the dark like a blind person. Not switching on lights, I crawled from bed and followed the dog down the hall to our living room, expecting to let him out into the fenced yard.

As I neared the stairs leading up from our front door, next to an iron railing that divided the stairwell from the living room, I pleaded, "Lord, when are you going to heal my eyes?"

The words came from about a foot above my head. A man, invisible in the blackness, stood in front of me and answered. Verbally. Not in my mind. Not to my heart. To my ears.

I knew immediately who spoke: Jesus himself. After all, John 10:4 affirms that His sheep know His voice.

We can tell much about people from their tones—whether a person is anxious, angry, happy, or teasing, loving, or friendly. From Jesus' voice I learned two unforgettable lessons.

First, He has complete confidence that He *is* the supreme authority in the universe. When He speaks He knows He *will* be obeyed. If He orders a response to a prayer, that request *will* happen.

The other attribute I heard was total, full, pure, intense, powerful *love*. Love far above any we find from human sources. Jesus *is* love. Unblemished, impossible to diminish *love*. Impossible to fully describe.

There's no way a person can forget that spectacular voice. God didn't need to create the drama of my lost glasses for an important and unforgettable lesson, but I suspect He enjoyed the process. God surely loves drama and a good story.

That night in the dark Jesus asked me one simple question: "Can I do with you what I want?"

"Yes, Lord." I joyfully lifted my hands toward Him as I replied from a full and willing heart.

Our conversation was brief but powerful. After He left, I was awestruck. Jesus himself had visited and spoken to me! Me, an ordinary person.

Jesus did not heal my eyes that night, but it didn't really matter, because He gave me a fresh vision of Him. Decades later, I'm still awestruck at what Jesus did in that short meeting.

Thirty years after Jesus spoke to me, during an operation for cataracts, permanent lenses were implanted in my eyes. I can see clearly without washing spots from glasses, wiping away fog on winter mornings, or wondering where I left the lenses when I toppled into bed. Surgery, yes, but still a gift from God.

I never did let Turk outside that dark night, but he must not have minded. He wouldn't have understood the part he played in God's setting me up for a lifetime blessing . . . that of knowing the character of Jesus evident in His voice and receiving fresh spiritual vision.

His Eyes Pierced My Heart

JULIE B. COSGROVE

In 1994, eighteen ladies crowded into the living room of my family's summer home along the river. Some sat on couches, others on the floor with their legs folded underneath them and Bibles balanced on their knees. Around us were scattered chocolate candy wrappers, bags of potato chips, cans of soda, and prayer journals.

I was anxious about this weekend. Lately, I'd felt this unquenchable thirst to bask in the fellowship of Christian women. This retreat meant everything to me. I'd hoped the women at this church we'd just joined were enjoying it. I so wanted them to like me.

The retreat leader said, "Everyone, please close your eyes."

She played the old familiar hymn about walking in the garden with Jesus in the cool of the morning. Then she said in a hushed voice, "Now picture yourself in that garden with Jesus."

The room swelled with silence. I watched as many of the ladies bowed their heads and clutched their hands together. I am sure most of them went there in their minds.

I didn't.

Instead, my prayer walk took me to the riverfront below the bluff where the summer cabin nestled. I can still recall what happened as if it were displayed before me on an HD screen.

I walked along the bank under the canopy of century-old cypress trees. The water rippled with sunlight. Two squirrels chattered and dashed in a spiral around one of the trunks. This summer place held my heart. Throughout my life, it had been the easiest spot for me to pray. God was always there, as if waiting by appointment. That's why I'd invited the ladies here, hoping they would also feel His presence.

But on my prayer journey that day, I didn't enjoy the peacefulness I usually felt as I strolled along the riverside. My footsteps shuffled through the dewy grass. I barely lifted one heel before stepping forward with the other foot. The stride resembled my life—treading through molasses. The weight of the world pushed onto my shoulders. Both arms wearied from the fight to keep my family members' heads balanced above the waters of despair. My heart felt laden with life.

Our household included a typical woe-is-me hormonal teenage boy overloaded with school, band, soccer, and Scouts. My husband had lost his career and was holding down two menial jobs to make ends meet. Then there was me—a working mom who collapsed from exhaustion each night about midnight and then rose at six to do it all again, and again.

We shared a car since we couldn't scrape enough together to repair the other one. I had our budget down to a science of menu planning around the coupons I clipped. In other words,

I was no different from thousands of other working moms. But it still was an enormous weight to bear.

I stopped to gaze out onto the water and held back the tears. This was where so many of my childhood memories rested. Days of giggles and splashing, of learning to dive and swinging from ropes over the river while friends yelled, "Jump!"

Simpler, worry-free summer days. Oh, how I longed for them.

Then, out of the corner of my vision, I saw something move at the dock. A man. What was he doing here? Was he fishing?

My palms became clammy. The other women were in the cabin on the bluff above me. I was all alone. Should I run back up the path or stomp toward him and confront him for trespassing?

I did neither. Instead, I stared. Something about him was different. This guy wasn't dressed in jeans and a T-shirt as I'd expect any fisherman to be wearing. He wore a pure white robe and tan sandals. His hair was shoulder-length brown with a slight curl in it. When he half-turned in my direction, the sunlight streamed through the cypress branches and haloed his head.

Jesus was on my dock. My heart clenched. The Lord of my life had chosen to appear to me—me, a worry-burdened woman who wasn't praying as often as she should, nor finding the time to read her Bible daily.

He held out His hand.

In a transported instant, I was toe-to-toe with Him. Tingles spread from my chest to my fingertips. Was this real?

"You only have a few minutes left." The retreat leader's words filtered through my dream scene.

The words leapt from my tongue. *Lord, I need you.*

I looked into His face and, in rapid fire, began to spout off every question in my mind, every angst that dangled in my heart, and every thought that churned in my stomach.

Jesus' eyes filled with mirth. His grin widened. He laid His hands on my shoulders in a gentle grasp.

The warmth of His touch seared me. I gasped and held my breath, my mouth open. Words jammed in my throat.

It sounds cliché, but mere words cannot describe the love shining out of His eyes. They pierced my heart. The earth stood in silent stillness, out of time and space, as we exchanged looks. His smile penetrated my soul and caressed it. Every ounce of exasperation, doubt, and fear melted from my mind, flowed to my feet, and seeped onto the dock and into the river.

Then He drew me to Him and hugged me. I put my head on His chest, just for a moment, and felt His love wrap around me like a towel warmed from the dryer. When He released me, He again peered into my face—all the way to my core.

As I looked into those amazing eyes of Christ—and I honestly can't tell you their color—I began to fathom just how completely my Savior cares for me. It was the most precious gift anyone could ever receive—to come face-to-face with unconditional love.

Jesus' eyes glistened. He never said a word. He didn't have to. His expression revealed all that needed to be said.

That moment by the riverbank, I truly knew, down to the bottom of my soul, what it means to say, "Nothing can ever separate me from the love that is in Christ Jesus" (see Romans 8:39). Whatever life throws at me in the future will dim in comparison to the pure peace I felt in His presence.

"Now I understand," I whispered. Tears flowed down my face. A smile stretched across my cheeks.

He nodded and turned to walk away. Then He was not there.

Yet He was. And He has been ever since.

My mind returned to the living room with those eighteen ladies. When it was my turn to reveal what I'd experienced, all I could say was, "He hugged me."

It was so deeply personal that I squirreled it in my heart and told no one—not even my husband or my mother. It was years before I could even speak about it.

Then one day God whispered to my soul, "It's time. Release it. Share it. You won't lose any of its power if you do. Trust me."

And so I have. Amazingly, the preciousness of that occurrence has not diminished in discussing it with others.

At first, I worried that people would think I was loony or delusional. But instead, I've witnessed their tearful smiles and nods. My story has blessed others and bolstered their faith, just as it does mine.

Sure, life can weigh me down. We still struggle financially. At times I'd rather fast-forward to tomorrow and forget today even existed. My mind worries about family and friends. Utter helplessness clouds my heart when I hear that someone has been diagnosed with cancer or has lost a loved one. I shake my head at the news of trafficked girls and corrupt business practices. I'm disturbed at how self-absorbed so many people are today, and I wonder where our nation is headed.

In my quietest moments, I've questioned why my Lord would die for someone as flawed as I am. As Paul admitted in his letter to the Romans (chapter 7), I have the desire to do good. I promise God I'll change. However, because of my fleshiness, I don't always carry it out. At times I've doubted that I have the faith armor to endure what lies ahead.

Then the memory of that prayer walk returns to calm my soul. My heart fills with wonder that He could choose to forgive me once again, and that His love will never fail. Undeniable peace spreads through every pore of my being. My angst melts in the warmth of that memory as I fall to my knees in gratitude.

If the understanding I received that day on the riverbank is the only insight Jesus gives me this side of heaven, it is more than I need and abundantly greater than I deserve.

The Hound of Heaven

JAMES STUART BELL

During Christmas vacation, my friend Joe and I were home from our colleges and decided to use the time to pursue our ever-revolving smorgasbord of psychedelic drugs, Eastern religions, and occult phenomena. Joe wanted to go to the Jersey Shore to visit his friend Steve, a fellow traveler in the New Age world before it was known as New Age.

The Christmas holidays can drag, and I eagerly accepted, looking forward to a change of venue, deep discussions on the nature of reality, and some drugs to heighten our perception and provide some background fireworks, so to speak.

At this point we had only a faint notion of the reality of the living Christ. So far in my quest for a direct experience of God, oneness with the universe, and self-transcendence, I had only bumped into one herald of the Gospel. On Thanksgiving break the previous month I had run into an old high school friend at a local hamburger joint and shared my "spiritual" experiences with him, hoping he, too, would want to benefit from a higher consciousness.

As we munched on french-fried onions, Bill looked pensive and told me that another guy, John, who had also attended our high school, had become a Jesus freak and had an interesting story.

I had been raised in a devout Roman Catholic family but had turned my back on Christianity after high school. Our religion teacher had told us there were many ways to God, and I was fed up with the seeming hypocrisy and uptight rules I had experienced while remaining a Christian adherent. I wanted to taste the fruits of unbridled freedom and self-fulfillment that others were pursuing in the late sixties.

So I drank deeply of these new philosophies espoused by my fellow college students and many of the college authorities.

I was, nonetheless, intrigued by Bill's referral. I had heard vaguely of the Jesus People and knew they were countercultural like me—living in communes and talking about peace and love. Many of them looked like what we imagined Jesus to look like and also like the Indian gurus and political revolutionaries I was following. So perhaps we had some things in common.

I called Joe and told him that John had embraced this spiritual way that differed from the bland legalistic faith we had inherited.

Joe and I hadn't seen John since he had been expelled from our high school after his sophomore year. We agreed that a visit to "compare notes" on our spiritual quests would be worthwhile and even entertaining.

Joe grabbed a thick paperback of occult-like mystical experiences titled *The Morning of the Magicians* to give to John. I called John and gave him a bit of my spiritual background, we hopped into the car, and we lightheartedly said, "We'll tell him God sent us."

In actual fact God had!

When we arrived at John's door, he was not hospitable. He had the predictable shoulder-length hair and overalls of a Jesus freak. And I knew by looking at him that he was a transformed person. But he would only speak to us through the screen door. And when we tried to give him our book to help bridge our different experiences, he looked disgusted and told us it was from the pits of hell.

It wasn't exactly a loving approach, but John knew he was in spiritual warfare when he encountered our darkness.

To pacify him I told him that Jesus was a good guy, a reincarnated perfect master . . . or some sort of Eastern gibberish. His eyes bore right through me as he refuted this assertion with the words of John 14:6: "Jesus answered, 'I am the way and the truth and the life. No one comes to the Father except through me.'"

The Word was like a sword that quickly shut me up.

We coaxed John into a ride with us and he told how he'd been out of his mind on a huge dose of LSD and was completely lost. He'd encountered a group of young Christians in a park, they prayed for him, and he immediately came off his drug trip. He explained how Jesus came into him and changed his life. John also spoke in tongues to us, and Joe and I could not deny that this had supernatural origins.

John told us how he was drug free through the power of Jesus. I was ambivalent about that. I didn't particularly like the aftereffects of drugs but couldn't imagine giving up what I thought would be the sublime transcendent experiences they afforded.

So when Christmas break came a month later, though I had been impacted by our encounter with John, I had not experienced any supernatural encounters of a Christian kind and was dealing with an oppression I couldn't describe.

At the Jersey Shore, Joe's friend Steve brought us into his house and I picked up a record album titled *War in Heaven*. In the message of this album, the bad angels win. It gave me negative vibes, but then Steve suggested we take some hallucinogenic mushrooms, and we talked about peyote proponent Carlos Castaneda.

We walked along the shoreline and decided to eat more mushrooms. That was a mistake. Suddenly we were flying on an intense mind trip, and for our own safety, a friend of Steve's gave us permission to stay at an apartment near the water. As the evening wore on, we locked ourselves in the bedroom, snuggled into our sleeping bags on the floor, and stared at the pitch-black darkness.

A Beatles song on the stereo, "Eleanor Rigby," asked where all the lonely people belong. A sudden wave of my nothingness invaded the darkness. I felt alone in the universe. Who was I, and what was the purpose of my life?

This was supposed to be the Buddhist way—achieve the annihilation of self to merge with the cosmos. But it felt like a dark, horrible abyss from which I might not return.

Suddenly, against the backdrop of the inky darkness, I saw a stunning cross with the suffering Christ upon it. He looked at me with a mixture of sadness and compassion. I realized I had something to do with why He was nailed there.

Though I couldn't see Joe, I turned and said to him in a low voice, "Jesus claimed it all. Do you think He was right?"

Joe turned on his side and didn't answer. Maybe he was asleep. Years later Joe said he did hear me, and in his mind and heart he answered, "Yes."

"The Hound of Heaven"—the term for Christ from a famous poem by Francis Thompson—kept pursuing us, and within six months we had both surrendered our lives to Christ.

Though this was a drug-induced experience, God used it to make me consider the finished work of Christ on the cross for my sins. In my darkness and nothingness He died to become my light and my everything. And in my quest for supernatural experiences, the One who was previously hidden condescended to reach me in the way I desired.

From Stillborn to Miracle of God

DENNIS E. HENSLEY

I'm really, really sorry, Mr. Hensley, but your baby is dead."

"Dead?" I echoed, my eyes widening in shock. "How can the baby be dead when it hasn't even been born yet? This can't be true."

The doctor put a hand on my shoulder. "I cannot hear a heartbeat. I've had three nurses and another doctor listen, and they can't hear a heartbeat either—only your wife's. I've hooked up two different fetal monitors to the child inside the womb and both have flatlined for five minutes each. I don't know why this happened, but I have to tell you: The baby is dead."

I collapsed into a hard plastic chair in the hospital hallway. I was thirty years old, and my wife, Rose, was twenty-nine. We had a three-year-old son who was as healthy as could be, and for the previous nine months everything had seemed normal during each of my wife's checkups. We had the nursery all ready for the new baby, although we didn't know ahead of time if it would be a boy or a girl. I had gone through childbirth classes again so I could be with my wife during the delivery. Everything was as it should be . . . except that now, on the day of delivery, the physicians and nurses were telling me our baby had died.

"What . . . what do we do . . . about this?" I rambled.

This obviously was not the first time the doctor had had to answer that question. His responses were so automatic—almost as if he were following a script—that I had to resist feeling offended.

"First, I think you need to be the one to go in and tell your wife about the situation," he said. "After that, maybe you can call some relatives or close friends to come and spend the next few hours with you. It may be another five hours before we actually extract the body."

Extract the body? That was my child he was talking about.

"Then I'll need you to sign some forms so we can perform an autopsy to determine the cause of death. I know that sounds harsh, but it may help us learn something that could save another child's life in the future. Other than that, it'll just be a matter of comforting your wife as much as possible until after the procedure."

Procedure? Extract the body? Was he afraid to say *birth* or *delivery?* Did this have to be so clinical? My heart was broken, and I still had to go in and tell my wife about—what had he called it?—*the situation.*

I stalled by first calling our parents. We were in Muncie, Indiana, where I was finishing work on a PhD in English and teaching at Ball State University. Our relatives were all back in Michigan, but they said they'd leave as soon as possible to come to be with us. The drive would take six hours.

When at last I went in and told Rose the news, she nodded and then starting crying. She said, "The baby hasn't been kicking for the past two hours. I've been worried something terrible had happened."

We held hands, wept, and were silent.

In time, friends from our church arrived, and one dear lady named Sandy Scott convinced me to go to the hospital chapel with her to pray.

"I know you, Dennis," she said. "You teach Sunday school, you serve as the missions treasurer, and you even help with evening children's church. I can't help but think that the Lord is putting you and Rose through this tragic ordeal for a higher purpose. I don't know what that can be, but I want you to trust Him. This is all part of His plan."

I honestly could not see how the death of an innocent child could serve God's purposes in my life, especially when I felt as helpless and as hollow as it was possible to feel. I had served a year in Vietnam as an army sergeant, so I knew about losing close friends. But I felt those men had died serving a great cause. This baby . . . well, it had never even had a chance to accomplish anything.

Nevertheless, I prayed for spiritual strength. I also prayed for physical strength so I could comfort my wife when I was with her during the removal of the child. That came all too quickly, and before I knew it, I was dressed in green scrubs and seated next to my wife's head as they prepared her for the "extraction." Unlike when my son had been born, they turned away all of the mirrors so I would not have to witness the birth of our deceased baby.

The attending nurse opened the registry book. Next to HENSLEY, I saw her print STILLBORN.

My heart seemed to stop beating. At that moment if I could have given up my own life for my child, I gladly would have done it. In that instant, I sensed a voice saying to me, "Now you understand how it feels."

And yes, probably for the first time in my life, I truly understood the sacrifice the Father had made in giving His only Son to die for my sins. It was a revelation that would stay with me forever.

The doctor and two nurses had been working for about fifteen minutes when the doctor suddenly said, "That's impossible."

Then the attending nurse said, "That baby just wet on you. An infant cannot have bodily functions if it's dead. That baby is alive!"

My wife was too exhausted to follow what was going on, but I heard every word as clear as a bell. I stood and took two steps toward the medical team, but the other assisting nurse raised a hand and said, "Please sit down, sir. And keep your mask on."

The doctor whirled around and placed our baby—a little girl—on a table nearby. He inserted a tube down the child's throat and then squeezed on a rubber bulb syringe on the opposite end. The baby's lungs filled with air. The doctor released the balloon, and her little lungs deflated.

"Here, take over," he ordered the attending nurse. "The baby can't breathe on her own. Keep a slow, steady rhythm." He turned to the other nurse. "Call for Dr. Jasper. I need backup in here *now*!"

He then returned to caring for my wife. Within two minutes another doctor and two more nurses arrived. They told me I'd have to leave.

"But what is going on?" I demanded. The doctor would not say. However, the attending nurse winked at me. She walked over to the registry book, and as I watched, she crossed out the bold printed word STILLBORN and wrote above it MIRACLE OF GOD.

Pushing me toward the door, she said, "The baby is alive but has a faint heartbeat. She's too weak to breathe on her own, so we're doing that for her. We've called Riley Children's Hospital to send a special ambulance to take her to Indianapolis. I don't know if she'll make it, but I do know that your *dead* daughter is now alive."

Dazed, I stepped into the hallway. When friends asked what happened, I said, "She's alive."

"Rose was dying?" they asked.

"No, no," I said. "The baby. It's a little girl. She's alive. They say she's very ill, but she's alive."

My friends tentatively shouted with joy, tempered by the fact that our daughter still might die. They stayed by me, and after an hour we were told that Rose had been taken to isolation because she had lost a lot of blood. They let me go in to see her, but, exhausted from the ordeal, she wasn't even wholly conscious. I let her rest and sought one of the doctors.

"I have no explanation for it," the doctor said. "Five of us pronounced that baby dead, and two different fetal monitors confirmed no heartbeat. I don't believe in miracles, but I have no medical explanation for this."

The special ambulance arrived, and a pair of trauma nurses shared the task of pushing air into our child's lungs during the ninety-minute ride to Riley. For the next twelve days, I made the hundred-mile round-trip to see my daughter each afternoon, and each day she grew stronger. After only two days, she was breathing on her own. She began to suck a bottle after one week. On day twelve, my wife, son, and I got to bring her home. The diagnosis was that she had been born with a complete heart block, and even though she had survived, her heart would never beat more than just every other time on its own.

After the celebratory hoopla calmed down and an endless stream of visitors stopped coming to our house to see the "miracle baby," I had time to be alone. And it was then that my prayers bordered on bitterness.

Yes, I was overwhelmingly grateful that my daughter was alive, but I could not help but feel puzzled, even angry over the fact that God had played such a sick joke on my wife and me.

"Your baby is dead. Whoops, uh, not really." What kind of a warped God would inflict such needless agony on a couple who had served Him well?

During my times of soul searching, Sandy Scott's words continually came back to me, echoing her message that God had a purpose in all this. I also remembered hearing those words: "Now you understand how it feels."

After a full year had passed, our family doctor, a woman in her early thirties, became pregnant with her first child. We were truly happy for her. Each time we brought our children in for checkups, we asked her how she was doing, and she always exclaimed that she was in great health and excited about her child's arrival.

We were stunned when word reached us that on the day of her delivery, her little son lived for only nine hours. The umbilical cord had wrapped around his neck in the womb, leading to complications that took his life. We grieved for our doctor.

Then the situation grew worse. When we called for our next appointment, we discovered that our doctor had given up her practice, gone into a deep, emotional depression, and wouldn't even come out of her house. She considered herself a failure as a mother and as a physician. No one could convince her otherwise.

Suddenly, I realized the importance of the words, "Now you understand how it feels."

I wrote a long personal letter to our doctor. I explained exactly how she was feeling—hollow, impotent, lonely, useless. I talked about anger and bitterness and frustration. But I also talked about love and purpose and service. I quoted lines to her from 2 Chronicles 16:9: "For the eyes of the Lord run to and fro throughout the whole earth, to show Himself strong on behalf of those whose heart is loyal to Him" (NKJV).

I ended the letter by saying, "I now know why I had to be hurt so severely a year ago. It was so I'd be able to talk to you. There is a purpose for pain. You are an excellent doctor, and during your career lifetime you will deliver a lot of babies. Not all of them will live. When the parents turn to you and say, 'You don't understand,' you'll be able to say, 'Oh, I do, I truly do,' and you'll be able to minister to them in a way other doctors do not.

"I'm sorry we both had to be hurt so deeply, but I'm also honored that the Lord would call us to such a level of service for Him. You *must* go back to your practice. We all need you."

Two days later this woman called me.

"You were the only one I would listen to," she said. "No one else understood. And because of your letter, yes, I'm going back to my career as a physician."

That was many years ago. Recently I saw in the paper that she has just retired after serving many decades as a family physician. Oh, and my daughter Jeanette? She had a pacemaker put in when she was thirty-two, and she's now a schoolteacher in Elkhart, Indiana, with a husband and two healthy kids. That's pretty good for a baby who was declared dead even before she was born.

Yes, the nurse had written the truth: MIRACLE OF GOD indeed.

A Heavenly Painting

SANDRA MERVILLE HART

As I drove to my friend Ella's house on a warm September evening, tragic events Ella had recently faced weighed on my mind. Two years earlier she'd lost her daughter, Jessi. About three weeks later her husband, Bob, had died of a heart attack. These deaths struck a crushing blow to the family, friends, and the whole church.

When Jessi died, Mark, a talented artist and former member of our church, created a beautiful painting celebrating Jessi's life. It captured her joy of living, her enthusiastic spirit. When Bob died, Mark portrayed Bob and Jessi walking along a serene beach. Through Ella's intolerable grief, the painting brought the comforting reminder that her husband and daughter awaited her in heaven.

Besides grieving these deaths, Ella had undergone several illnesses the past year and now had a badly broken wrist. I imagined Ella felt a bit like Job.

Ella greeted me at the door with a smile, but her eyes were filled with the same familiar grief. The beautiful painting of Jessi hung prominently on the wall. Not seeing Bob's painting, I asked about it.

"I don't have it." Her shoulders sagged. "I took it to get it framed and when they finished, I didn't have the money to pay for it. The store sold it by the time I returned for it."

This news broke my heart. How could the store owners have done this? Since the topic obviously brought pain, we spoke of other things, though Ella mentioned it twice more before I left.

The loss of the painting after all the tragedy struck me deeply. It left a burden that would not ease.

When I ran into Amy, a co-worker of Ella's, a couple of days later, I asked if she knew which store might have sold the painting. She hadn't heard anything about it.

Driving home in the dark, I prayed, "Lord, should I pursue this?"

As soon as the words left my mouth, Proverbs 3:27 sprang into my mind: "Do not withhold good from those to whom it is due, when it is in your power to act."

I'd never memorized this verse, so I realized it had to come from God. Something must be done to restore this painting to Ella.

The next day I met with Roni, who leads the women's ministry at our church. She was shocked to learn of the missing painting and wanted to help. We agreed that I would call Ella's sister, Debbie, for more information.

Unfortunately, Debbie didn't know which craft store Ella had chosen to do the framing. She explained that Ella had left the picture at the store months past the deadline for pickup. Even if we knew which store, they would be unlikely to retain records of specific transactions for so long.

I relayed this information to Roni. She asked Mark if he would re-create the artwork, and he graciously agreed to do so free of charge. He simply requested a photograph of the original. We were thrilled that Ella would have her painting.

But now we had to deal with the cost of framing again. Ella's broken wrist prevented her from working her main job or her side job of cleaning homes. I decided to recruit a large number of people to provide the frame and I thought of the choir. Ella had been part of this ministry for years but hadn't been involved lately. I hoped to include this compassionate group in blessing Ella.

Lloyd, our worship minister, enthusiastically supported the whole worship ministry donating to this cause. He wanted to frame the painting and present it to her before Christmas. I shared with the choir, worship band, and tech crew what had happened to the painting and how I learned of it. Over the next two weeks, an offering collected for this cause totaled $315. Any money beyond paying for framing would go toward a gift card for Ella.

Debbie provided a photo of the original painting and we waited. Our artist friend had been blessed with a huge job for a major organization and would squeeze our request in when he could.

By the beginning of December, I wondered if the painting would be done in time to present to Ella at the last choir rehearsal of the year. When I went to the craft store to check prices, a sign stood in front of the display: *Any items to be framed by Christmas must be in by December 9.*

I discussed this with Lloyd. We still wanted to give the gift to Ella before Christmas. Jessi had died in January, and Bob had died in February. We wanted to avoid these anniversaries.

If Mark finished, we would present the unframed painting to Ella before Christmas and take it for framing afterward.

I continued to pray that the painting would be done before the ninth, but it wasn't. Mark hoped to finish it over the weekend. This would be three days before the last choir rehearsal. Having the painting would give Ella a semblance of peace for Christmas.

But we heard nothing by Sunday.

The next time Roni talked with Mark, he mentioned he often had a certain person frame his work. He might be able to get the painting done and framed for choir rehearsal on Wednesday.

Getting the gift ready wasn't my only concern. I was a bit worried about how the painting would affect Ella. She had been understandably broken for months and months. Certainly she would cry when she saw it. Would it break her heart all over again? Or would it bring a new healing, a new understanding that her church family suffered with her?

After praying for her, I recalled the drive home in the dark when I asked for God's guidance. Remembering His instantaneous response calmed me. God knew what He was doing. He knew the outcome. For all I knew, Ella may have been fervently praying for the painting's return.

Mark planned to deliver the painting to church on Wednesday afternoon, framed. I brought the money to church and waited. He called to say some spots needed retouching and he would not be there until four. And he said he was paying for the framing.

Since the choir had taken up a special collection specifically for this, we decided to put all the money raised on a Visa gift card for Ella. It seemed that even this larger amount was God's plan. He knew what she could most use.

Rehearsal lasted long but Ella was not there. Since she lives near the church, Lloyd called and asked her to come over. When she arrived, I explained that the choir wanted to bless her. Lloyd brought the wrapped gift forward.

Ella tore open the wrapping and stared at a portrayal of Bob and Jessi walking together along the peaceful shoreline, their shadows mingling to become a cross behind them. It outshined even the original.

Ella began to sob. She hugged me and thanked me.

"God did this," I explained. "He was the One who said we should do this."

Ella could barely speak. When she calmed a little, I explained that Mark wouldn't let us pay for the painting or frame, so we had something else for her. She sobbed harder.

"Ella, everyone in this room is your church family. We're your brothers and sisters. Your choir family has been very generous. Here's a gift card for you."

Ella's happiness delighted all of us. After rehearsal ended, a few gathered in front of the painting. Someone asked, "Where is that supposed to be?"

With a peaceful look on her face, Ella replied, "It's heaven."

Ella later posted a photo of the painting on Facebook. She commented, "I didn't think I could feel this happy."

God used many people to bless His child in this instance. He could have done it without us. He could have caused the original painting to come to light somewhere in Ella's direct path. But that's not how He chose to do it. He wanted to use more than fifty people to accomplish His will, knowing what a blessing it would be to those who gave as well as to the one who received.

Speaking With Divine Assistance

KRISTI EDINGTON

My mom, who has the biggest heart for all creatures, great and small, was in a terrible accident. She was helping the animal control and highway patrol try to catch a small dog that was running astray on a busy highway. Cars were swerving and trying not to hit the dog. The patrolmen had closed down the traffic on the highway temporarily in an effort to prevent a larger accident.

Mom's car was parked on the shoulder of the exit ramp. She was standing in front of her car with dog treats trying to lure the dog off the roadway. That is when someone failed to slow down as he approached the stopped traffic. By the time he realized traffic was still, it was too late for him to brake.

He swerved toward the exit ramp, trying to stop, but slid sideways off the highway. He lost control of the car and was going approximately seventy miles an hour as he hit my mom.

She flew over his car, bounced off the trunk, and landed on the exit ramp.

Mom was flown by medical helicopter to a trauma hospital nearly an hour away. Soon family members from all over the country were making their way to the hospital because her survival chances were slim. We tried to avoid the thought of being without Mom and prayed constantly for her to recover. She just had to survive; we still needed her too much!

Mom survived, but she faced an uphill battle. Her broken ribs had punctured a lung, and the lung would need time to heal. A ventilator was inserted to help her breathe. As Mom drifted in and out of sleep, she tried to speak to us. Many of the family members had such a hard time understanding her that we gave her a pen and paper to write what she wanted. Most of what she wrote was illegible or confused. Since she was on so much pain medicine, she frequently had hallucinations and mixed-up thoughts.

Slowly the lung tissue healed, and the doctors removed the ventilator tube from her throat. Mom had difficulties breathing on her own, but the doctors hoped it would be easier as the day progressed. She couldn't talk to us; we figured her throat was sore from the tube and her struggle to breathe.

That evening, the doctors put the breathing tube back in. She was able to calm down and rest and breathe much easier. She didn't require the ventilator, just oxygen through the tube. As long as the tube was down her throat, though, she was unable to talk. She still tried to form words, but it was very frustrating. Mom had always been quite the character; we couldn't imagine her not being able to speak.

Two weeks later, the doctor said Mom's vocal chords must have been damaged when the emergency personnel put the ventilator tube down her throat. Now the surgeons needed to put a tracheostomy in her throat. She would not need to be on a ventilator, just have the tracheostomy with an oxygen mask over it.

Several days later, the speech therapist came in and gave her a speaking valve for the tracheostomy. Normally, with a little practice, a person can speak normally with the valve. Mom could not make even the slightest sound! That left her even more frustrated, if possible.

A few days later, another specialist came to visit her, an ENT (ear, nose, and throat) doctor. He put a tiny scope in through her nose to look at her vocal chords. As he was looking through the camera lens, he directed, "Say A" or "Say E." He repeated this over and over. But she could not make the slightest sound. I could tell she was trying hard to say each letter, but nothing came out.

After the doctor removed the scope, he sat on the chair next to Mom's bed, grabbed her hand, and held it as he told her the bad news.

"Your vocal chords are paralyzed. To make sound, they have to vibrate. Yours not only don't vibrate at all, but they are paralyzed closed. That is why you are having such a difficult time breathing without the tracheostomy."

He said that down the road he could do a surgery to reposition one of the vocal chords, and though she would never be able to breathe without the tracheostomy, the surgery could possibly give her a slight, raspy voice.

Not the news we wanted to hear.

The next day, I spent most of the afternoon and evening with Mom. She was so lonely and depressed. Mom had severe damage to her right leg and would never be able to walk on it again. As I sat at her bedside trying to make out the words she mouthed, her frustration level was at an all-time high. It seemed like she faced one disappointment after another.

I probably had the hardest time of anyone understanding her, and had even made up a ring of cards with common words or phrases on them to help her communicate. She was crying and couldn't find the words she was looking for, and so threw the cards across her bedside table. So I asked her to write what she wanted. I felt so bad for her but could do little to help.

She wrote for me to pray to Jesus with her. I was to tell Jesus that she was okay with not ever walking again, but that a woman needed her voice. She knew the suffering Jesus went through, and He would understand her suffering.

I bowed my head, took her hands in mine, and prayed to Jesus, just as she wished.

Suddenly, she jerked her hands away from my hands and wrote, "Pray louder. You have to pray loud enough for both of us. Besides, there are so many other needy prayers all the time; you have to stand out to Him. Pray very, very loud."

So I did just as she wished. I'm quite sure I could be heard all the way down the hospital hall!

"Jesus, you know Mom doesn't expect everything to be perfect," I shouted. "You know her heart and that she can live without walking if she has to. But you also know she can't tell others about your mighty power and about your miracle of saving her life if she can't communicate. . . ."

I kept my eyes closed—not just because that's what I normally do when I pray, but also so I couldn't see anyone stopping by the room and glaring at me for being so loud.

My voice began to get hoarse, but I continued. We thanked Jesus for sparing her life and told Him we felt blessed beyond belief with that answer alone. We knew that only His hands had saved her. I asked Him for the strength to help Mom hang on, to not lose faith even when facing a bleak future. I begged Him one last time for her to be able to speak once again so she could share all God's work with others.

After shouting "Amen," I told Mom it was late and I had to get home.

She hugged me and wrote, "Thank you. I love you."

On the way home, I spent most of the hour-long drive listening to Christian radio, praying, and wiping the tears from my eyes. I knew my mom would survive, but how would she be able to live without a voice? Anyone who knows her would say that she is one of the wittiest people they have ever met. With this injury Mom could still be a clown and a goof, but the things she said just made her actions funnier.

I finally made it home and had a restless night trying to sleep, but worrying about Mom instead.

Early the next morning, the phone rang. My heart raced.

No one calls me this early; something must have happened to Mom.

I ran across the room to the phone. When I answered, instead of the typical "Hello," all I could say was, "What's wrong?"

"Hello." The whispery voice sounded like one you'd hear in a scary film.

Surely a prank caller or wrong number.

"Who is this?" I demanded.

The eerie voice spoke again: "I'm your mother."

"My mother can't speak, now who is this?" I snapped.

That's when the voice on the phone became more familiar. My mom's nurse, Amy, explained to me that when she came in the room and was changing the date on the dry erase board, she had asked Mom how she was, as usual.

Mom had responded, "I am doing great. Can you really hear me or have I totally lost my mind?"

Amy was startled by the previously silent patient. Mom then told her how I had prayed so loud that nurses had come in later and told her that they would have made me leave for being so loud if I hadn't been praying! She couldn't talk then, but when Amy came in, she surprised herself when actual words came out.

That afternoon, the ENT doctor returned. He asked her how she was talking, and she told him of our prayer. When he looked at the vocal chords again, he asked her to say different letters and sounds. He did these three different times.

Finally Mom looked up at him and said, "Can't you hear me?"

"Yes, I can hear you," he replied. "But I don't know how. Your vocal cords aren't vibrating at all."

Her vocal chords were still one hundred percent paralyzed.

He just stood there, scratched his head, called in another doctor to look down the scope, and finally said, "This is truly a miracle. I have never seen this happen. Paralyzed chords do not make sound!"

Mom spent four months in the hospital and met doctor after doctor who did not believe her vocal chords were totally paralyzed—otherwise she would not be talking. Before long her normal voice returned. She told people, "You just can't shut a woman up!"

With all of her determination, she has managed to walk again with only a cane and a brace on the entire right leg. Four years later, doctors are still amazed to see the work of the Great Physician and Healer. Her vocal chords remain paralyzed and she still requires a tracheostomy to be able to breathe, but we are all thankful for the gift Jesus gave us by answering a very loud prayer.

I Am Your Warrior

C. F. SHERROW

My mission trip to Kenya had been over for nearly six months and I was definitely feeling overdue for a spiritual "jump start."

Thank heaven, the group that sponsored the Kenya trip had arranged a weekend retreat for the following spring in Red Cliff—a beautiful, rustic center northwest of Pueblo in the Rocky Mountains—even though scheduling anything for the mountains in March was iffy.

I'd gotten the vacation days I'd requested, which didn't always work that well. My request included an extra day before the retreat to get ready, pack, and make the three-hour drive, then return on Sunday. Nice.

A minor monkey wrench appeared: The weather forecasters predicted a big snowstorm due to arrive on Wednesday. Seriously? Those guys always had to be so dramatic.

No sweat. It would be here and gone by the time I was supposed to leave on Friday. As long as I left by noon, I'd get to

Red Cliff by suppertime and check in with time to spare. I might even have enough time to stretch out my road-weary muscles for a bit.

The typical spring snow showed up right on time, bearing huge, fluffy wet flakes. But this storm took residence. By the time it was all over, we had nearly two feet of snow on the ground, not counting the drifts sculpted by the wind. My office actually closed on Thursday, since the only traffic moving through town was the four-wheel-drive kind. I appreciated the day off, but panic threatened to set in. I'd already paid for the retreat. I'd already gotten vacation days from my limited bank of time. I just had to get to Red Cliff!

Dig, dig, and dig some more. Lift and toss. The snow was so wet, heavy, and thick I had to remove it in three layers, through many sessions. I wasn't the only one trying to clear away the mess. The whole neighborhood was out scooping, digging, and shoveling down to the sidewalk. The drifts by my driveway were waist-high or more, and not melting. This stuff was too deep and wet for most snow blowers to handle safely.

On Friday morning, I was somewhat relieved to see that someone from the neighborhood had plowed a single track down the other side of the street. Once I navigated that, it would simply be a matter of getting out onto the plowed main streets.

I managed my exit later that day with plenty of time to spare.

Along with the other participants, I was soon walking along plowed paths from dining hall to cabin and back again, between high walls of snow that kept the temperature below freezing.

The spiritual warmth during the teaching sessions more than made up for the pervasive physical chill. Intense times of worship and prayer were alternated with simple conversations around the fireplace. People were receiving words from God, encouragement, even visions.

Departure time was downright depressing. At least the roads were clear and the drive uneventful. However, I did not look forward to going back to work on Monday as I dragged my suitcase to my bedroom and unpacked.

I considered staying home instead of attending our regular Sunday evening Bible study, but decided to go. Maybe I could make the "retreat glow" last a little longer. Besides, most of the study folks had been at the retreat—we could at least compare notes and rejoice at the good things that had happened.

Praise and worship was more powerful than usual, probably a holdover from Red Cliff. God still seemed to be among us.

Suddenly, my peace evaporated. Anguish hit me like a football lineman. I knelt, doubled over, face nearing the floor, weeping.

You see, nearly four years earlier I had started dealing with the spiritual and emotional issues I faced from my childhood, when a cult had gotten ahold of me. I knew some demonic forces still hung on.

They could not possess me, but the harassment was relentless as they lied to my heart, telling me that I was damaged beyond repair. My mind knew better, but my heart despaired.

And that night I realized they were taunting me again. My spiritual restlessness and discouragement from the past few weeks began to make sense. How could I ever get beyond this?

"Jesus, you know I would get rid of this stuff if I could." I sobbed. "But I can't!"

This confession was incredibly difficult. I was used to taking care of myself, solving my own problems. But this—this was way beyond my strength and my ability to fix. Did anyone have what it would take to heal me for good, inside and out? Did God really care?

Then I saw Him. Jesus came toward me. He was riding a white horse, and He was wearing the shiniest silver suit of armor I'd ever seen. It wasn't like the pictures you see of Him coming back to earth dressed in white robes. If it had been, I would have thought that well-known image was straight out of my own mind.

He was my knight in shining armor? Never saw that one coming! I continued to watch His approach, curiosity overcoming doubt. Then He stopped.

"I am your warrior."

That was all. It was enough. Those four words convinced me that I didn't have to heal myself. I didn't have to attack my problem alone. Jesus was fighting for me. My warrior knight would continue to fight for me until the battle was done. We would get through this together.

My Daddy God

ANGELA DEAL

At eleven years old, I hadn't heard the saying, "When it rains, it pours," but that's what was happening in my world. My family and I had recently moved. While I was trying to adjust to a new school and a new set of friends, an unexpected blow rocked our family. I learned of it late one night when I tossed and turned in my bed, unable to fall asleep. I heard Dad telling Mom that he was leaving our family.

I wondered how we could mean so little to Dad that he could abandon us so easily, but then, on the day that he left, I looked into his eyes and saw brokenness. My heart grieved for his pain and I prayed, "Jesus, Dad is lost and confused. Please help him."

On the heels of this turmoil, I began noticing I couldn't run very far without getting out of breath. A few times, I even blacked out. The doctors said I'd been born with a hole in my heart, and surgery was the only way to correct it.

"Open-heart surgery?" I gasped. "No! I won't go through with it!"

At least when Dad had left, I knew I wasn't alone. My mother, sisters, and I were in that situation together.

However, I wasn't prepared for this bombshell. I felt very alone in this new, scary battle. The strong, loving presence of a father calming all my fears would have been a healing balm, but I didn't have that.

Sometimes I felt angry. Sometimes I felt life wasn't fair. But mostly, I was just really scared.

What if I die? I thought in horror. *What if I'm never normal again?*

I wanted to run and hide and pretend it all away. But of course I couldn't. I kicked and screamed. I panicked and cried. I blamed my mother and I even blamed God.

When I walked down the long, cold corridors of the hospital for tests, my fears rose with the strange odors of disinfectants and ammonia wafting through the air. Between doctor appointments, I fretted and worried and cried in desperation, "Jesus, please help me!"

I never heard His voice. I couldn't even feel His presence. But then, one day while walking home from school, a Bible verse popped into my mind: "A father to the fatherless, a defender of widows, is God in his holy dwelling" (Psalm 68:5). It grabbed my attention and I couldn't shake it from my thoughts.

Is Jesus trying to tell me something here? I wondered.

Hope and anticipation rose within me. I hurried home and slipped into my bedroom. Then, finding my Bible, I turned to the concordance in the back and looked up the words *father* and *orphan* and found three other verses that jumped out at me:

"I will be a Father to you, and you will be my sons and daughters, says the Lord Almighty" (2 Corinthians 6:18).

"Do not take advantage of the widow or the fatherless. If you do and they cry out to me, I will certainly hear their cry" (Exodus 22:22–23).

"You [have] received the Spirit of adoption by whom we cry out, 'Abba, Father'" (Romans 8:15 NKJV). *Abba* is an Aramaic word most closely translated as "Daddy."

Wow! Is Jesus trying to tell me that God can be like a father to me and will help me when I call out to Him? Could I really mean this much to Him?

I knew I wasn't exactly an orphan, but Dad's absence in my life left me feeling like one. Certainly, I'd be thrilled to accept God's invitation! So sitting on my bed, I bowed my head, closed my eyes, and in simple childlike faith, prayed, "God, I would like you to be a father to me just like you promise in your Word. I don't know how you would do it, but I'd sure like it if you could." After several moments, I finally opened my eyes as peace washed over me.

I soon learned that when God makes a promise, He always acts on it in His perfect timing. At that time in my life I had a newspaper delivery route. One day, while I delivered the paper to my waiting customers, a boy with a black eye and fresh blood smudged across his face approached me.

"Hey, you!" He rubbed the back side of his hand across his dripping nose. "Give me your bike."

"No," I stammered, gripping tightly to the handlebars. "My dad will come after you if you take it." The words tumbled out of my mouth before I could stop them.

Oh, I shouldn't have lied! I panicked. *Of course Dad is nowhere around to help me out!*

"Oh yeah?" The bully shot back, his face turning bright red. "Well, I don't care!"

He inched closer to me and made a fist with one hand.

Then I remembered what Jesus had taught me: *God is my Father! He will hear me if I call out to Him!* With sweaty palms and a pounding heart, I prayed silently, *Oh, God, please help me!*

Suddenly, out of nowhere, a deep masculine voice spoke sternly.

"Boy! You leave her alone!"

The boy's eyes grew wide. Then, like a scared rabbit, he dashed away. I let out a long, shaky breath and glanced around to find the person behind the voice. An elderly gentleman stood in his yard near me.

"Are you okay?" he asked.

"Yes," I nodded. "Thank you."

I suddenly realized that even though I hadn't actually seen God, He had heard my cry for help and was there to defend and protect me through that elderly gentleman!

I grinned.

"Wow, God!" I whispered. "Your promises are true. You really *are* a perfect Father. You are *my* Abba, Father! Thank you!" My heart bubbled.

As the day of my operation loomed closer, I carried this new revelation about God close to my heart. Oh, I was still scared. But now I had a Father to lean on, and I could draw strength from the comfort He offered so freely.

When the time arrived for the operation, I felt God wrap His arms around me in the form of peace and hold me tight. He whispered into my heart that He would never leave me or forsake me. And He never did. He helped me ignore all the strange hospital smells and frightening appearances of other sick children, and He helped me to pull through the operation with flying colors.

While I was recovering in ICU, a fresh wave of fear swept through me. I began crying, and God lovingly spoke, "Don't cry. Everything's okay." This time, though, instead of speaking through an elderly man, He spoke through a little child lying next to me—a voice so sweet and angelic that it immediately calmed me down.

Years have passed since those days, but the lessons of my youth taught me very early in life that I don't have to see God with my physical eyes to know He is near. When I open my heart to Him, His presence *will* surround me wherever I go.

And because Jesus' death on the cross was to restore mankind's fellowship with God, I know that Jesus will do for others what He did for me those many years ago—gently guide whoever thirsts straight into the arms of a loving *Abba, Father.*

Jesus Called Me by Name

ANITA ESTES

In my sophomore year of college in the early seventies, I dated a high-energy "geodesic dome–building hippie" who wanted to take off for Europe with me. I was young and adventurous, so I dropped out of school and joined the ranks of the counterculture.

Since I'd gone to Catholic school all my life, this offered me freedoms I never dreamed of before and sounded like the opportunity of a lifetime. Unfortunately, after a week in Switzerland, he let me in on his plans to go to India. Though I was naïve, I wasn't stupid enough to go there without vaccinations, so we parted company.

I met a band of wandering travelers and hitched a ride with them in a van to Greece. It was an audacious journey as we passed through a few military controlled countries, but miraculously we made it safely to Athens. There I met more hippies, and we hopped a boat to an island in the Mediterranean.

All the while I tried to run as far as I could from God. But He was watching out for me, and the first day in Crete I ran straight into a Jesus freak. A skinny young blond approached me and handed me a leaflet.

"God wants you to change your lifestyle," he said.

I thought that was pretty nervy of the guy to say, but I listened anyway. "He sent Jesus to help you. He loves you."

I grabbed the leaflet and smiled, but on the inside I ridiculed him.

Doesn't he know that's all a myth?

I tossed the paper aside and ran toward the Mediterranean, gazing at the sunshine playing on the water.

This scene would be a great inspiration for a painting or poem, I mused. I jumped into the water with some other friends. It felt wonderful: cool, refreshing, and intoxicating. We splashed around for a while, then I plunged underwater.

This was so different from the murky Atlantic, where you could hardly see a thing. I was enchanted by the sparkling sunlight penetrating through the water. Yet something was troubling me—that annoying Jesus freak. I tried to ignore his words and dove deeper.

As I swam along the bottom, beliefs about my new way of life kept popping up. I'd explored different avenues in my life as an artist, a poet, a writer, and an honor student, and now I was traveling the world at the ripe old age of nineteen.

Yet it all seemed kind of meaningless.

I tried to cover my pain with all sorts of things that deep inside I knew weren't good for me. Thoughts about what the guy on the beach said kept plaguing me, but I felt that a religious lifestyle was way too restrictive. I had lived it for years and now longed for freedom.

Anyway, I wondered, *does God even exist? Even if He does, how could He have a Son, Jesus?* I knew my catechism answers, but they were outdated.

As I swam around thinking, I heard someone whisper my name, "Anita."

It was a gentle, soothing voice, but I thought it was one of my new companions. I glanced around underwater and saw no one, though I felt someone's inviting presence.

Looking up toward the surface, I saw streams of light breaking through where the voice emanated from, and I popped up for a minute. Glad for the oxygen that filled my lungs, I still felt confused as I glanced around and didn't see any fellow travelers.

Who had called my name?

Pushing the thought aside, I took another breath and plunged back down. I loved the underwater world and could stay down for longer than most people.

As I swam, I continued to wrestle with some of my feelings. If God loved me and the world, why was it such a mess? Why did my boyfriend want to leave me stranded in Europe?

We had agreed not to go to India because it would have taken more time to get vaccinations. While both of us were into yoga and meditation, he decided he wanted to pursue these avenues in India. I had taken several college courses on Gandhi and India and knew the poor conditions that existed in most of the country. I thought he was crazy to go and would probably wind up getting dysentery. Still, my heart ached and I felt lonely without someone by my side.

As I continued swimming, I lost track of time, enchanted by little schools of colorful fish and undulating seaweed. Engrossed in my thoughts and exploits, I probably stayed down for much longer than I should have. Then once again I heard the voice call louder and with some urgency, "Anita, come here!"

The water was dark, but streaks of light penetrated it. The light beckoned me, but I struggled to respond because part of me wanted to investigate further.

I started feeling cold, so I decided to swim to the top. As I broke through, I gasped for breath and had a hard time breathing normally. I didn't realize how long I'd been down under. It took me a minute to recover from feeling dizzy and lightheaded.

I looked around, but none of my buddies was close enough to have called me. Since they were swimming too far away for me to yell to them, I waved my hand to attract their attention. Someone swam in my direction.

As the friend headed toward me, I wondered why one of my buddies had played this name-calling game with me. Stranger still, a warm feeling engulfed me, and I felt bathed in light.

When my friend arrived, he asked, "Where were you?"

I heard the concern in his voice.

Confused because I thought he had been messing with me, I replied, "Swimming underwater." After a moment I asked, "Why did you call me?"

"I didn't call you." He scrunched up his nose.

I laughed and shook my head, scattering droplets of water from my hair. "Well if you didn't, then Peter did. I heard my name very clearly, 'Anita, come here.'"

He shrugged his shoulders. "Honest. It wasn't me, and Peter got out of the water a while ago."

I was mystified. I had heard my name very clearly, but I dropped the subject and swam back to shore. Inside my head now, the voice called me again. This time it sounded strangely familiar, like a voice I recognized from childhood.

What's happening now? I wondered. I couldn't shake the feeling that something very important had just occurred.

As I headed toward the beach, I felt really different—clean, like someone had touched me with liquid light that penetrated my darkened heart. The bewildering thoughts that had plagued me a few minutes earlier vanished. But I couldn't help thinking, *Who called my name?*

Other thoughts surfaced. *What would have happened if I stayed down any longer? Could I have drowned or been hurt? Maybe that voice saved my life.*

The whole incident seemed strange, but the feeling of peace remained. It reminded me of when I was a little girl. When I used to come home from church, I'd be singing like a bird. I was so happy then, not the dark, brooding person I was becoming. Yet for now, I felt a great peace and sense of holiness envelope me.

When I got out of the water, the godly presence grew stronger and I felt wrapped in warmth. I sat on my blanket and began to draw, but my pencil seemed to have a mind of its own. At first I drew a body shrouded in seaweed-like bands. Then a face filled with compassion and inviting eyes emerged. As if on its own, my pencil wove a crown of thorns on His head and nail-pierced hands. When it was finished, I couldn't believe my own eyes. There before me was a picture of Jesus with outstretched arms!

The sun grew warmer all about me and light penetrated my soul. Waves of cleansing washed over me. As I sat on the beach contemplating what just happened, my spirit stirred. I took up my pen and wrote about the incredible experience of cleansing and forgiveness while passing through the waters of baptism.

I had been baptized as a child in the Catholic Church but knew very little about its true meaning. Yet somehow I felt so clean, washed from my sin. I bathed in the light, letting it penetrate into my body, mind, and spirit. I wrote on, while staring at the picture of Jesus I had drawn.

That night I kept thinking about His face with the crown of thorns. Though I sensed His presence, I felt as if one of those thorns pierced my heart. It was both beautiful and disturbing, but I just couldn't give up the lifestyle I was entrenched in.

Slowly the peace faded, and I returned to the life I was living. Yet I continued to write poetry about Jesus during my trip, and I had other less dramatic encounters with Him.

When I returned home to the States, the incident faded from my mind until I remembered my writings about my baptism experience.

I submitted the poem, and it was published in a Christian magazine at the college I attended. Though I continued my education at another university as an art student in upstate New York, I wrestled with depression and darkness.

Then one day a friend invited me to an InterVarsity meeting. When the man spoke, I sensed the same Spirit as I had felt in Crete. After a few months, I finally answered the call. Day by day I came to know the Holy One.

I realize now, without a shadow of a doubt, that Jesus rescued me from what could have been a tragic fate. Whether He kept me from bodily harm in the Mediterranean, I don't know. However, that wasn't as important as the work He did in my spirit. Jesus saved me while I was yet a sinner and baptized me in His cleansing waters. It just took me a couple of years to catch up with the transforming work He had already done. Jesus called me by name.

Visitor at the Foot of the Bed

TAMMY BOWERS AND LEE BOSWELL

Alone in my hospital room, I cooed at my new baby girl—so sweet. As I tried to scoot out of the small bed, a stabbing pain sliced across my C-section incision and I froze. Seconds passed before I inched back down. The position I reclined in would have to do for now. Looking at my daughter's beaming face, I smiled back. Pain couldn't erase my joy.

"Do you know you're a miracle baby? Almost two months late, yet perfectly healthy." *Except for your odd stretchy skin.* I gently tugged my newborn's forearm and lifted her pink skin up two inches. "Very strange. But you're still a beauty with your midnight blue eyes and long blond hair."

Most babies are born with dark blue eyes. Would my little girl's lighten as she grew, turning sapphire like mine or green like her father's?

My throat clenched at the thought. My husband didn't even know he had a daughter.

My smile dissolved and tears threatened to overtake me, but I fought them off. Today wasn't a day to mourn or dwell on my shame, which was ridiculous in the first place. I had done nothing wrong. I had tried everything I could to help him. The doctors wouldn't listen when I told them how after his injury my husband ate pain pills like popcorn.

If only they'd heeded my concerns.

No! I shoved away the hurt. Today was a day to celebrate. I had much to be thankful for—a healthy boy turning four the next month, and a one-day-old girl who survived seven weeks too long in my womb.

"You just weren't ready to see the world, were you Tamara Dee?" I stretched my thumb and forefinger apart to measure the length of her hair. "I bet it's four inches. It had extra growing time."

I had never seen a newborn with such long hair. It was amazing. "As soon as I get you home, I need to take some pictures."

"Knock, knock." A tall nurse swept into the room dressed all in white. Shoes, stockings, dress, and nurse's cap. Even her hair was white. Well, platinum. "I need to take your baby for skull x-rays."

"Skull x-rays?" An odd expression passed over the nurse's face. If she hadn't been staring me in the eye, I would have missed it.

The nurse forced a smile. "Nothing to worry about. Just some routine testing." She slipped Tamara from my arms and swooped her out of the room.

Routine testing? My heart thundered in my chest. I was only twenty-five, but I knew there wasn't anything routine about x-raying a newborn. Tamara wasn't my first baby, and my twin sister had two children. None of them had needed x-rays. What was wrong with my daughter?

Lumps filled my throat as I struggled to breathe. How had my life fallen into such shambles? And why had it happened? Nice church girls didn't have to flee in the night from their husbands with a son in their arms and a baby in their belly.

I closed my eyes and forced myself to breathe deeply. As slowly as I could make my lungs move, I exhaled. "Please, Lord, heal my little Tamara Dee. I place her in your hands. Fix whatever is wrong. I can't endure more heartache. I need you. I'm all alone, Jesus, and can't bear this by myself."

For several minutes, I poured out my soul to the Lord Almighty.

My mattress depressed and the squeaky springs echoed in the stark room. Someone had just sat on the end of my hospital bed. It was probably Mother or Daddy, but even if it wasn't, I didn't care who heard my prayers. My daughter needed help so I kept praying out loud.

The person sitting with me didn't speak, but he or she must have joined me in prayer, for a warmth filtered into my legs. Soon, peace bathed me and my heart rate slowed. My whole body tingled. As joy seeped back in, it chased all fear away. Little Tammy Dee would be fine. Somehow I knew it.

After a deep exhale, I opened my eyes to thank my visitor for praying with me. But no one sat in the deep crevasse at the foot of my hospital bed.

The dent smoothed out as the unseen person rose. Again the old hospital bed squeaked.

My heart thundered, but this time not from fear over losing my newborn.

Jesus. He was here with me.

I closed my eyes.

Once again the bed moved as Jesus sat back down.

"Oh, Lord, thank you for coming to comfort me. I don't have to go through this alone." I hiccupped out the words, unable to stop the tears from streaming down my cheeks. "Thank you," I repeated many times as more tingles filled every pore of my body. Love soared through me.

"Jesus, you're at the end of my bed? You care enough about me in small-town Taft, California, that you'd come and wait with me? Unbelievable! You are magnificent. Hallelujah!" Not once did I open my eyes, as if doing so would send Christ away. "I know you're always with me, but this time you showed me in a real way. I am so grateful. I am in awe of you. I love you, Savior."

And I love you, child. The words penetrated my mind, bringing more tears. I couldn't wait to tell someone. Who would believe me? Jesus actually sitting on the end of my bed did sound a bit farfetched. "I know the truth, and I praise you with my whole heart."

Although invisible, Christ sat with me for thirty minutes until my boisterous nurse whooshed back into the room.

"I'm amazed. Your little princess didn't cry once through the whole process. I've never seen anything like it," she chirped.

As I opened my eyes, my gaze shot to the foot of the bed. The indentation lifted as Jesus stood. When the nurse returned Tamara Dee to my arms, my attention veered to her and I grinned. "I'm not surprised. She's a miracle baby."

I kissed her soft forehead and caught a whiff of that wonderful newborn smell.

"The doctor will be right in to talk to you about the test results." The six-foot nurse glided out of the room, shutting the door behind her.

No doctor arrived for hours. Most mothers would have gone

into hysterics over the wait. Not me. I enjoyed a beautiful morning with my daughter. No worry or dread. Just the warm peace lingering in my soul.

At noon the doctor pushed into my room, a paper towel in her hands. "Well, your daughter gave us a little scare." She perched at the foot of my bed where Jesus had been. The mattress depressed and the old spring echoed through the stark room. "First of all, everything is okay."

The doctor dried her hands while gazing at me.

"During my rounds this morning, I examined Tamara Dee and could not find a fontanel—a soft spot. Babies are born with two. They accommodate the rapid brain growth in infants. Without soft spots, the brain will push the eyeballs out of the sockets, blinding the child. It can also cause mental retardation. To confirm the diagnosis and get ready for Tamara's future medical needs, I ordered skull x-rays. I just finished reviewing the films with the radiologist."

"It's good news." I couldn't contain another grin.

"Yes, it is. She has two tiny soft spots. One's right here." The doctor pointed to an area near the top of my baby's skull. She tossed the paper towel in the trash and stood over us, roaming her fingers over Tamara's scalp. "Even now, I can't feel it, but the x-rays don't lie. I think her fontanels began closing because of how far overdue you were."

"Is that why her skin is so loose?" I pulled it up again. Tamara didn't even notice.

"Yes. The epidermis started deteriorating. Don't worry, though." The doctor patted my hand. "Tamara's skin will return to normal and her brain will develop normally."

"I know." I told the doctor that Jesus had come to sit with me, as evidenced by the squeaky bed moving up and down.

The wary expression on my doctor's face revealed her skepticism. She didn't argue or ask any questions as she squeezed my shoulder and exited the room.

My gaze dropped back to precious Tamara Dee in my arms, her wide eyes staring up at me. "When you're old enough, baby girl, I'll tell you all about Jesus. He sat on my squeaky bed and waited with me because He loves us. You and me. I know you'll believe my story."

The Man in the Long White Robe

DAVID MICHAEL SMITH

Lynne stood in front of the medical clinic alone as a cold, brisk December wind rushed through her, cutting her troubled soul into tattered shreds. The voices in her head debated and accused, questioned and tempted, reasoned and screamed.

Then one voice silenced the others and calmly said, "I love you and I will always love you."

After a time of silence so deafening that Lynne feared her pulsating eardrums would implode, the other voices returned and prompted her to enter the stark cement block building for the scheduled procedure. After all, the voices reasoned, it would make everything right again.

Two hours later she left, empty and grieved, but convinced she had made the correct decision. After all, wasn't this legal? Endorsed by our lawmakers and magistrates?

Now she had her future back on track; life was no longer derailed. A "mistake" had been erased, removed as if it had never happened, and her family would never know.

But something felt awful inside. She wanted to get sick.

Fifteen years passed, and with it several new boyfriends, college, a husband, a divorce, and a job transfer to the Delmarva Peninsula for a fresh start. Lynne made the journey with her two chubby cats, a few boxes of possessions, and the clothes on her back. It was time to rediscover who she was and where she wanted to go with her life. The future, hopefully, would be a better destination than the past.

Over the years, particularly during holidays and on the anniversary of her abortion procedure, she affectionately remembered the small soul who once resided within her womb. Confused at the time about the legitimacy of its human existence, she now believed what was inside her body had in fact been *life*. Life as evidenced by biological and medically observable facts such as a tiny pumping heart only a month after conception and moving fingers and toes. This haunted her. She felt soiled and ugly from the inside out. How could she ever forgive herself?

While adjusting to a simpler life on the eastern shore, she met a man named Lance. They began to date and love blossomed. Lance, although not a holy or perfect man, regularly attended church and believed in God. Lynne joined him every Sunday, and eventually they married in the blessed company of family and dear friends.

Shortly thereafter Lance sponsored his spouse for the first of two weekend retreats that would ultimately change Lynne's life.

After the first retreat in Maryland, which started on a Thursday evening and ended with Holy Eucharist three nights later, Lynne found herself falling in love again, only this time with a

Man named Jesus. She began to read her Bible every morning, attend Bible study once a week, listen to Christian music, participate in church ministries including altar guild and teaching Sunday school, and most noticeably, do the Lord's work in the mission field, outside of the church walls.

Lynne and Lance often visited the nearby retirement home and brought cheer to the lonely residents. They read the Bible to elderly men and women, many near the sunsets of their lives, and prayed with them, but mostly just talked and listened.

One lady once tearfully looked upon Lynne as she was leaving and spoke with a quaky voice, "When I look at you I see an angel." And she meant every word.

As the years passed, the couple continued to walk with the Lord, growing in the Savior's love and joy, yet something discomforting always nagged at Lynne. Down deep she was still burdened from carrying the heavy load of guilt and sadness over her aborted baby. If only she could somehow take it back, make it right.

After years of infertility battles, God blessed the couple with a son, but only after they first adopted a daughter from China. Slowly but surely they were walking closer to Jesus and learning to be obedient to the Holy Spirit's will and wisdom. And now they were the joyful parents of two miracle children.

Soon Lynne, following the encouragement and footsteps of her husband, began to take healing ministry classes at church. The program included nearly two years of classes, taught on video by Francis MacNutt, a former Roman Catholic priest with national appeal and credibility, and his wife, Judith. Their teaching impacted Lynne, and after she completed the courses she became a prayer minister at the church. Every Sunday healing ministers would welcome people in need to their kneelers, lay hands on them, and pray for their petitions. Healings and miracles were documented at the church as the Holy Spirit flowed over those encounters.

"Soaking prayer" was a powerful tool the ministers used to combat more serious issues, such as inner healing and demonic confrontation. Soaking prayer appointments usually lasted an hour or longer. Lynne and her husband participated in this special ministry and witnessed great improvements in the recipients' lives.

Around this time, Lynne learned about weekend retreats for women and men who had been harmed by the sting of abortion. They were called Rachel's Vineyard weekends, the name based on Scripture from the prophet Jeremiah. A nearby Christian-operated pregnancy crisis center posted a brochure in the church narthex announcing a Rachel's Vineyard retreat in Ocean City, Maryland. Lynne felt that she needed to attend this weekend. So she signed up, said good-bye to her family, and checked into the seaside hotel where the retreat was being held.

The entire weekend was a blessing. Lives were forever changed, and the balm of forgiveness transformed many from struggling to redeemed. At one very poignant moment, women were asked to name their aborted children. Most felt a strong sense about the child's gender, male or female, and Lynne believed her child had been a baby boy. She named the child Isaac, after the godly man from the Old Testament.

After that weekend Lynne felt lighter and happier, but something was still not quite aligned. The very next week, she scheduled soaking prayer during the evening—not for another hurting saint, but for herself.

Three women—Lynne and two parish members trained in healing prayer ministry—met in quiet supplication and love on a Tuesday evening. They sat in a triangular configuration just in front of the altar. A large wooden cross with a porcelain figure of Jesus Christ hung above the scene. Peace reigned over the sanctuary. And then with Lynne closing her eyes, the ladies laid hands on her and began to talk to God.

Lynne lost all concept of time. Had she been there moments, minutes, or hours? She was relaxed, comfortable, and expectant. She heard Karen, one of the prayer warriors, say, "I sense Jesus is with us, in our midst."

And then it happened.

To this day Lynne isn't sure if it was a vision or reality, but with eyes closed she clearly saw a man with a long, white flowing robe approach her from a distance. She was sitting near a babbling brook alone, ashamed of her decision of twenty-five years earlier. She glanced up again and the man was closer. He looked familiar. . . . *Jesus!*

Oh no, it's Him, she thought, panicking. *He must be angry with me.*

She lowered her head, frightened and unable to meet His gaze.

Time passed. Lynne no longer heard the intercessory words of the prayer team; she was fully immersed in the vision with Jesus.

She sensed His presence, a light—an incredible shining, vibrant light—standing above her, but she dared not look upon the face of Christ her Savior and Lord.

Then . . . a touch. A man's hand, scarred in the palm, reached under her chin and gently raised her face. She opened her eyes and saw Him, Jesus, the living Lord of Lords and King of Kings. He was smiling. His soft, caring, and dark eyes met hers as the tears began to flow.

"Child, I love you and I will always love you," Jesus spoke reassuringly.

She remembered the voice—His voice and His words outside the clinic that day. It was Him! She was unable to speak, and He continued, "And Lynne, my daughter, you are forgiven."

Jesus held her in His arms while years of pain and suffering left her. The vision ended and once again Lynne was back in the church with her friends, still praying, full of grace and hope. But she was forever changed thanks to an encounter with the Savior and His eyes of healing—the Savior who continues to redeem and forgive today, just as He did yesterday and will continue to do tomorrow for His children across the globe.

The Stone Fireplace Miracle

EVELYN RHODES SMITH

I probably never would have admitted it, but I was a bitter woman . . . and had been for decades.

I hadn't been very old when my father had left my mother, my younger sister, and me to move in with Helen Johnson, a woman he met at work.

He left us destitute.

To support our family, Mom became our neighborhood washerwoman. In rain or snow, cold or hot weather, my younger sister and I delivered clean laundry to the neighbors who used her services.

Later, when Mom had a heart attack, our family was on welfare for a few months while she recovered. Even though I was very young when all this happened, I never forgot the name: Helen Johnson. And the fact that my father supported *her* family—not his own—gnawed at me. As a young child, I wept bitter tears over the misery and suffering we endured.

It was a tough life, and it became even tougher and scarier after my father tried to kidnap me.

I was nine years old the summer Dad came by our home and asked Mother if he could take me to the circus. My sister, who was six years old, was too young to go, he explained. He just wanted to take me.

I'd never been to a circus, so I begged Mom to let me go. She finally relented. I got into his car, but he didn't take me to the circus—he took me to his and Helen's apartment.

Shocked and frightened, I didn't protest.

But then I discovered my father was planning to take me to Texas with him, Helen, and her family. Something about Mom suing Dad for child support. I started kicking and screaming at the door until they let me out and I ran home sobbing, afraid that Dad was going to come and get me. For weeks, even after Dad was gone, I was still terrified of being kidnapped again and forced to live with him and *that woman*!

When I grew up, I praised my Lord Jesus for the kind and loving husband He had given me. But deep within, I still hated the woman who had broken up our home, and my heart was filled with bitterness. Almost daily, something triggered a memory and I would be thrust right back into my childhood years to relive the fear, anger, and pain.

Then we decided to build a new home.

Building a dream home muted the devastating bitterness I'd felt in my heart for a long time. Shopping for furniture, I had little time to reflect on Helen or my dad, my mom's humiliation, or other childhood experiences.

The neighbors in the subdivision were friendly, often stopping by to chat and get acquainted. One older neighbor, who introduced herself as Mrs. Mullins, became a regular visitor.

She lived down the street with her daughter and son-in-law. On sunny days, she and I walked together in our subdivision. She was quiet, not saying much about herself, but I found out she loved the outdoors and all animals.

My husband, Ted, and I had lots of pets. Dogs, a white rat, a skunk, birds, snakes, and whatever else we found injured and nursed back to health before releasing. Mrs. Mullins and I related on that level.

"She's really sweet; I look forward to meeting her entire family," I told Ted. "And she is a woman of faith, so we've begun sharing prayer requests."

Ted and I had been married for nearly twenty years at that time. We had both trusted Jesus as Savior in our early teens and were active in our church. Everything in our lives was covered with prayer—including the dream home we were building in this new chapter of our lives. I earnestly prayed that we would be happy in our new neighborhood and show the love of Jesus to others.

I reveled in God's goodness in allowing us to build this perfect house. Our home would have two fireplaces: a brick one downstairs and a stone one on the first floor. The stone fireplace had to be contracted separately since our builder did not have a stonemason on his crew. A handsome young man, Ray, came to our home to lay the stone.

I was at our construction site on most days helping with odd jobs, and Ray and I became good friends. He, a committed believer, had just returned from his church's mission trip to South America.

Ray told me about an incident that had happened on the trip, saying, "I don't know if you believe in miracles or not, but I saw it myself. One of our work crew fell from the top of a building we were working on and broke his neck. The Lord healed him, and he returned to work a couple of days after the accident."

I assured him that I, too, certainly believed that Jesus could heal! Ray and I began to share our time together in precious fellowship.

Listening to Ray talk about his friend's healing, I realized I needed a miracle in my own life. With details falling into place in the construction of the home, my mind was no longer as distracted, and it again returned to smoldering over the wrongs my father and Helen Johnson had done.

To assuage my grief and bitterness, I tried to be thankful for every blessing the Lord gave us. Therefore, I praised the Lord for Ray, the stonemason He had sent our way.

A few days before the fireplace was finished, Ray took his lunch break just as I arrived. He sat on the unfinished deck outside our living room area. The railings had not been put up and the deck overlooked a steep hill, about ninety feet straight down to the creek below. As Ray dangled his legs over the edge of the deck, I cautioned him to be careful.

"I will be—I'm just enjoying eating out in the woods."

Standing in the doorway behind him, I said, "Ray, I've never asked. What is your last name?"

He hesitated and then looked up and replied, "Johnson."

My heart skipped a beat. Ray Johnson?

Could he possibly be *the* Ray Johnson who was the son of the woman I had hated for thirty years? Helen Johnson's son? No, it couldn't be! Too much of a coincidence—*I hoped*.

"Ray, who is your mother?" I asked.

Ray didn't answer. He picked up his lunch and moved inside the doorway.

Then he stood with his back to the living room wall, and without looking at me, he replied, "Helen."

I felt as if my knees would give out—I had to sit down.

At that moment, Ted came through the door, carrying our lunches.

"Do you know who this young man is?" I demanded.

He shook his head.

"He is Helen Johnson's son!"

Of course Ted had heard her name hundreds of times—always with a heavy dose of anger and bitterness.

The events of the past instantly became real again as I looked at Helen's son. And I remembered the time I had seen him—the day Dad had kidnapped me.

Almost as if Ray were reading my mind, he interrupted my thoughts.

"I remember the kidnapping attempt, Evelyn. Your mother had sued your dad because he wouldn't pay the child support for you and your sister that was required in the divorce settlement. So he planned to move us to Texas to avoid monthly payments. I don't know how he got you to come to our apartment, but once you realized he intended to take you with us, you began screaming.

"I was afraid and hid in the kitchen. My mother placed a record on our phonograph hoping to calm you down, and the song 'You Are My Sunshine' filled the room.

"When your dad wouldn't unlock the door, you flipped the phonograph over. A bowl with my two goldfish was on the record cabinet and they came flopping across the floor right past me as I hid behind the kitchen wall. Fearing you might tear the whole apartment to pieces, your father finally unlocked the door and let you go. Our phonograph was broken beyond repair. We moved to Texas without you."

Hearing it from Ray, I relived it all over again. All of the agony, all of the pain.

I told Ray about the ruse Dad had used to get me to go with him—and the fact that afterward, I ran the two miles home without stopping. When I arrived home, gasping for breath and crying, I told my mom what had happened. She hugged me and cried, as well.

"I remember the damage you did to our apartment that day, Evelyn. That's why when you asked my mother's name I didn't answer right away. The last time I saw you, my two goldfish were dancing across the floor in front of me, and I was afraid you might push me off the deck!"

I couldn't help it—my tears changed to laughter, and so did Ray's.

I had not seen nor heard from Ray in the thirty years since that day. And now, he was standing in my unfinished living room! How glad and thankful I was that our blessed Lord had worked it out so that I got to know and love Ray *before* I found out he was Helen's son! Ray was weeping and so was I. The Lord was so good—all of my hatred and bitterness began to slowly melt away.

We talked for a long time that afternoon. When I asked about his mother and how she was, Ray dropped another bombshell: "You already know her."

Stunned, I waited for an explanation.

Jack and Anna Davis lived up the street from where we were building our home. Ray said that Anna was his sister, and their mother, "Mrs. Mullins," lived with her and her husband.

Since Mrs. Mullins had spent some time with me, she had soon figured out who I was. Ray added that his mother, Helen, had hoped and prayed I would *never* find out that she was the one who had broken up our home.

I wouldn't have if we hadn't bought a lot in the Thousand Oaks subdivision in Charleston, West Virginia. I wouldn't have had we not decided to have a stone fireplace in our home. I wouldn't have had I not asked Ray about his last name!

And I wouldn't have finally found peace had the Lord Jesus not orchestrated it all in front of our new stone fireplace!

The thought staggered me: After all those years, I was moving into the neighborhood where Helen Johnson Mullins would be living just a few doors away. *Oh, my precious Jesus-Savior, how I praise your holy name!*

Ray told me about the unpleasant life he had with my father. My dad was cruel and physically abusive, so Helen had finally left him. Then she had begun taking her children to church, where they all accepted Jesus as their Savior.

"My mother has prayed for your mother, your sister, and you every night since she got saved," Ray said. "She often wondered what happened to those two little girls and their mother, whose lives she felt she had ruined. Now she knows that our God has taken care of all of you, and she is finally at peace."

So was I. All the hatred my heart had held all those years was gone on that summer day.

We lived in that home for twenty-nine years, and I never passed by our stone fireplace without stopping to say, "Thank you, Lord Jesus, for meeting me here."

The Voice of Jesus

LYNNETTE GOLDY

I heard Jesus speak. Not only did I hear His voice, but I felt His healing touch.

It was 1971 and this eighteen-year-old, Bible-reading, rebellious Phillips University freshman in Enid, Oklahoma, closed the Bible and placed it on the desk next to her bed. I walked to the mirror and stared at the white spots on the back of my sore throat.

Oh great, I thought, *I've got strep.*

My roommate was already sound asleep, so I didn't bother her with the news. I said a quick prayer, "Jesus, you know I can't afford to have a sore throat. I can't miss school. Yes, this is a simple request, and why would you bother with my throat when you've got so many other things to attend to? Still, Jesus, please, will you heal my throat? Thank you, Lord."

I got ready for bed and decided to read another few pages of the Bible. Maybe it would help tire my eyes enough to fall asleep. I always tried to read a passage from the Old Testament, a psalm, and then a New Testament passage before going to sleep for the night. I didn't get very far this time—only the next few verses in Isaiah 30—before my eyes grew tired. I told myself I would continue my reading in the morning.

I was having difficulty falling asleep despite my weariness. And then I heard a voice behind me through the window, which was quite weird because we were on the third floor of the women's dormitory. Yet the voice was directly behind my head since my bed was centered against the window.

I heard one voice, and then I thought I heard two and maybe three, as if they were having a discussion. And then I felt the hands. Two warm hands pressed against my throat.

How can this be? What is going on?

The hands remained for several minutes, pressing ever so lightly. I looked toward my roommate, hoping she would wake up as she was tossing and turning in her sleep. I wanted to call out to her to let her witness what was happening to me, but I could do nothing with the hands pressed against my throat.

So I continued to lie very still and let the hands rest. I suddenly realized that these were the hands of Jesus! They comforted me, and I could feel the soreness in my throat gently subsiding.

Was Jesus answering the quick prayer I had spoken to Him before going to bed?

How much time had elapsed? It seemed like forever. Probably two to three minutes at least, and I wanted His healing hands to remain.

The next thing I remember is waking up still feeling the experience of the night in my body, feeling a little perplexed about what had happened to me.

My roommate was already up and getting ready for her first class. She was an early riser, like myself, which helped make us perfect roommates. The first thing out of her mouth was "Good morning!"

Her cheerfulness first thing in the morning always caught me off guard. I needed time to wake up quietly, by myself, in my own way. But she was a naturally cheerful person.

Not wanting to share with her yet about what had happened, I asked her how she slept and if she had a restless night. She replied that she did. I went to the mirror and looked at my throat.

It had no spots!

In my eighteen years of life, I had heard of Jesus healing people, believed in miracles, acknowledged that Jesus was healing when others told of miracles they had experienced, but had never had a healing myself until then.

I knew immediately that I had been healed by my Lord and Savior Jesus Christ. I knew then that He had answered my prayer.

I told my roommate what had happened, expecting approval and support. I told her about looking at my throat before going to bed and seeing the white spots. About the voice directly behind me through our window on the third floor. About the hands pressing against my throat. About my seeing her toss and turn in the night while all this was happening.

My roommate was absolutely elated.

We said a prayer together thanking God for what He had done and what He would continue to do in our lives.

Since that night, I've asked why God would choose to heal something so simple as a sore throat. Why would I hear His voice and feel His healing hands on my throat but not see Him with my eyes?

Perhaps it is because we live by faith, not by sight, as stated in 2 Corinthians 5:7. And because Jesus loves each of us. He cares about us. God speaks whether we listen to Him or not. Do not forget the miracles that happen in your life. You may not understand today why God works in the way He does. You may never know. Or it may take forty years, as it did me, to begin to better understand.

The Basement Visitation

DAVID S. MILOTTA

The day before Thanksgiving of my senior year in college, Jesus appeared to me. I was living off-campus in the home of a middle-aged wheelchair-bound polio victim. In exchange for free room and board, I took care of some of her personal needs, including helping her with bathing and insulin injections. My windowless, dirt-floor basement room was a converted cellar. Often water condensed and froze on my bare walls.

At the time I was in love with Sandy McLarren, whom I had met in Biology 101 class at Whitworth College. She was now attending school in Seattle at the University of Washington, pursuing a physical therapy degree.

The long-distance romance was emotionally taxing for me. I was wrestling with the future, wondering what God wanted me to be. My draft number had been passed over, so that threat was removed. My major was environmental studies with an emphasis on botany and geology. I marveled at God's majesty as I recognized the hand of the Creator by studying His creation. I thought of a career in the new field of environmental health.

My mother had told me when I was a young child that she had difficulty getting pregnant due to a tipped uterus. My parents had tried for ten years without conceiving. When she realized she was finally pregnant, she dedicated my life to the Lord's service. I always thought that was unfair of her, as it deprived me of my freedom of choice. I still wanted to be in control.

The night that Jesus appeared to me I felt God's tug in my life as never before. I didn't know what direction to take so I began to fervently pray.

"Lord, I don't know what to do with my life. What about my relationship with Sandy? How do you want me to serve you? Should I be an environmentalist? Please show clearly what direction you want me to take."

My prayers were so fervent as I struggled to surrender my self-will that I thought I was going crazy.

Then I became aware of a supernatural presence that was walking down my squeaky wooden staircase without making a sound. All my senses were on high alert as Jesus walked through my closed door, sat down on my chair, and revealed himself—turned on His appearance as if He were a light bulb.

I was so afraid I hid under the down comforter that was on my bed. He spoke to me with words that communicated a deeper meaning than what my ears could comprehend.

"Sandy is the girl you are supposed to marry. I want you to work for me full time."

I was too shocked to speak.

Jesus stood and His spirit passed through the wall.

The experience left me deeply shaken. Though I'd prayed about Sandy and my marching orders for life, I hadn't expected such a sudden answer delivered by Jesus himself!

Not everyone was on board for this dramatic turn of events.

I telephoned Sandy at her dorm in Seattle and enthusiastically exclaimed, "Jesus just appeared to me and said you were supposed to marry me."

Silence. When she finally recovered her composure over receiving such an unusual marriage proposal, she replied, "Well, He'll have to tell me, too."

When I brought Sandy to my home in Hawaii during Christmas break to meet my parents, my mother was so impressed by her that Mom started introducing her as my fiancée before Sandy had even accepted my proposal.

But she did, and soon a wedding date was chosen. The marriage was performed at Sandy's home church as part of the Sunday morning worship service.

In the years since that encounter, Jesus has been in close touch with me in other ways, too.

He has guided me through a successful ministry, thirty-eight years of marriage, and the rearing of two successful, God-fearing children.

Most often Jesus speaks to me in the everyday events of life: walking the dog, paddling in the ocean, windsurfing, and driving. But I'm still thankful that at that crucial time, Jesus came walking down my stairs and showed himself clearly to my senses.

You're Not. I AM.

MAIDA KEENY

The first time I heard the still, small voice, I was driving home from Bible study down a long, straight highway in southeast Texas.

We were new to the area. Within the past two years we had seen our fourth child born, declared bankruptcy, closed my husband's business, and left the only place we had ever called home for a fresh start in Texas.

But trouble followed us.

We were used to trouble. It started early on in our marriage and then escalated when we had three colicky babies in three years who grew into three hyperactive toddlers and then three ADHD school-aged children. There was always trouble. Trouble with teachers. Trouble with peers. Conflict at school. Chaos at home.

During his first semester of kindergarten, our second child broke another child's collarbone, threatened to punch out a substitute, and retired a veteran teacher. School started at 8:45, and by 9:00 each day, he was sitting in the principal's office. During our first parent-teacher conference for the second semester, his new teacher recommended that we see a pediatrician in town who specialized in behavioral issues. We did.

"Strife seems to rule our lives," I told him. "How do other families with three hyperactive kids handle it?"

"I don't know," he replied. "We know of no other families with three ADHD children that are still intact."

I wasn't surprised.

Marriage was hard, too. I went from living with an uninvolved father who only had strong opinions about politics to living with an emotionally high-maintenance man who had strong opinions about everything. After seventeen years of marriage, I was still having trouble adjusting to the stress level of our lives.

"I'm sorry," one of our counselors explained. "But they're stimulation junkies. It's the way their brains are wired. The same conflict that's throwing you off balance and making your life miserable is feeding your family's constant need for stimulation."

Lovely. Just lovely.

I had noticed that during the few times when we were riding in the car and everyone seemed to be at peace, someone would always pick a fight. Now I knew why. They were stir crazy. The quiet drove them crazy, and they needed to stir something up.

My mind needed peace and quiet, but theirs thrived on chaos.

I felt trapped. The frustrations of living in a war zone were overwhelming, and I was drowning in a sea of turmoil. At one point I packed a suitcase, hid it in the laundry room, and waited for everyone to go to bed so I could catch the next bus out of town. But when everyone was asleep, the crisis was over, and after a few days, I unpacked my suitcase.

Maybe the teenage years would be different. But no. After one particularly rough fistfight, I found myself cleaning blood off a doorpost—and it wasn't even Passover!

Today, though, I had other things on my mind. A new problem with one of our teenagers had reared its ugly head, and we were still reeling from the shock waves. We found a Christian counselor who specialized in our particular brand of dysfunction and started family counseling.

The more we uncovered, the more I realized how deeply rooted our problems really were. Our counselor recommended a psychiatric hospital near Houston and a specialist in town that we could see, but money was an issue.

Things didn't look good for our family, and my child's future was weighing heavily on my mind. The long ride home that day had given me time to think, but I was having trouble concentrating.

"What are we going to do about Matthew, Lord?" I said, not really expecting a response.

You're not. I AM. The words authoritatively flashed through my mind.

A few miles down the road it hit me. *Oh my goodness! That was the Lord!*

It had to be the Lord. It couldn't be my flesh. My flesh was looking for worldly advice. Put him in this school. Go to this counselor. Check out this hospital. But the Lord had other plans.

You're not. I AM.

He even used His name.

And His message rang true. I had been fighting my own battles and trying to figure out my own solutions to our problems for too long, and it was time to stop. Like Abraham, I was to lay my child on the altar and leave him there. God would do the rest.

I was to love him, care for him, and pray for wisdom concerning our daily issues, but when it came to Matthew's heart and future, God was in control. He would do the work that needed to be done in my child's life.

The following Sunday, I noticed several new tracts in a display case at church, picked up a few, and left them with my Bible on the coffee table when we got home from church that afternoon. I could read them later. Right now, there was lunch to fix and a dish to prepare for the potluck supper that evening.

Matthew was nowhere to be found when we headed to church later, so I left a note on the coffee table: "Finish your homework. Get ready for bed, and *don't* leave the house again!"

When we returned home that night, the note and tracts I left next to my Bible were scattered on the coffee table, and Matthew was in his room. We got ready for bed, but just as we were drifting off to sleep, Matthew walked in and stood at the foot of the bed.

"Mom, Dad, I've been saved."

"Saved?"

"Yeah. I read those tracts you left on the coffee table and realized that Jesus died for me. I'm saved."

You're not. I AM.

God was doing His thing. Just like He said He would.

Since then, each time I've heard the still, small voice, the words have been different, but the message is essentially the same: "You're not. I AM."

It seems to be God's theme for my life.

He will be the One who accomplishes what needs to be done in my life, and He doesn't really need my input. I don't have to try to control my circumstances or come up with my own solutions to our problems.

God is the Creator, and He has the power and resources to come up with much more creative solutions than my mind could ever conceive. My part is to simply lay the people and problems of my life on the altar and let Him take it from there.

The Night Jesus Walked
Into the Church

JANET DeCASTER PERRIN

I had seen a vision while in prayer. Women with black hair and brown skin stood on a beach with their backs to me, searching the horizon. They seemed to have emptiness in their hearts. I felt their longing and desperation for God, and I knew that one day I'd go to them and tell them about Jesus' love.

At the time I was given the vision, I had been praying and listening to a worship song that contained the verse spoken in Isaiah 6:8: "I heard the voice of the Lord, saying: 'Whom shall I send, and who will go for Us?' Then I said, 'Here am I! Send me'" (NKJV).

In prayer and worship that long ago day, I had responded in the same way that Isaiah had to the Holy Spirit's prompting. I said in my own heart, "Here I am, God, send me."

Then, nothing seemed to happen—for years. I enrolled in

and completed Bible school while my children were in their preschool and elementary years. An opportunity to serve in my local church arose, so I was privileged to take it.

But then suddenly, one day at the end of 2010, I heard these words: "The funding for part-time positions has been cut."

The economic downturn had not left our church untouched. The part-time staff position at my home church where I'd first volunteered and then worked as a staff member for three and a half years was gone! I had worked hard to develop and implement a new women's ministry in addition to other programs and pastoral duties.

How could losing my job possibly be a part of God's plan?

I would find out over the next two years.

As a full-time mom and part-time minister, I'd been so busy working while my kids were at school, then fitting in the household chores and kids' activities that I'd all but forgotten about the vision, which I knew was about short-term missions.

I'd dreamed of mission trips ever since I'd seen that vision. I'd prayed with confidence that one day I'd go, but busyness had crowded this out for a time. Besides that, it's easier to pray about things than to actually do them.

With more time available, I really began to seek the Lord, asking what door He intended to open next.

Unexpectedly, I received an offer to teach a Bible course I'd written as an adjunct faculty member at a local Bible college. I loved teaching, but toward the end of the semester I sensed that God had something new around the corner.

That's when the door to missions began to open. It wasn't to a place that I had expected, or at a time that seemed convenient, but I knew it was God, so I went. Perhaps if I had been employed at the time, I would not have been able to go.

I must confess that I had several fears and obstacles to overcome, but God was faithful to help me obey His call.

I was invited to be a team member to the Dominican Republic with RAIN Ministries Global Missions. That is where my short-term mission dreams began to come true.

One particular night on the trip stands out as a time when I witnessed Jesus touch people in such a powerful way that I will never, ever forget it. We were in a small church that held a few hundred people at most on the upper floor of a very humble building.

The local pastor was a wonderful man of God who had been part of our leadership training conference and had invited our team to his church. He and many local pastors of all denominations had been fasting and praying together for their city since a RAIN team had previously visited their region. We didn't realize that this pastor had invited a local deaf congregation to join our meeting that night. His faith in God's ability to heal was so strong that he had the front rows reserved for these dear people.

We arrived at the church, and soon the worship started. I was quietly praying for the service when I felt strangely sorrowful. *What's wrong with me?*

I could only silently weep as I listened to the worship and then the sermon in that little Assemblies of God church in Barahona, Dominican Republic. I should have been filled with joy because God had fulfilled my dream of missions, but I just kept crying.

I happened to be part of the prayer team, and we sat in the chairs on the left side of the altar, where we could see the worship team, the preacher, and the congregation.

Another team member was preaching that night, and his topic was holiness. He begged the church to come back to the holy fear and reverence of God. He called us all to live in holiness each day.

As he preached, I continued to sob. My spirit was so grieved by the prospect of any sin that lingered in the corners of my own heart that I was undone. I wept in repentance, followed by the pure joy of receiving God's forgiveness. For at least an hour during worship and the preaching I could do nothing but cry. Finally I fell to my knees on the floor in front of my chair and tried to remain inconspicuous behind a sound system speaker.

I felt something in the room that night that I can only describe as perfect love. I was stifling sobs, burying my face in my hands as I continued to pray for the meeting. As the sermon on holiness continued, the overwhelming love I felt increased. The presence was palpable, although not physically tangible.

Soon I noticed that the entire congregation began to quietly weep. Slowly the tears spread from the back of the church toward the altar. A holy presence seemed to sweep in the back door of the humble little church and continue rolling through the crowd to the front. I felt such a great sense of love in my own heart that I wasn't sure I could bear it.

This is what heaven must feel like, I thought.

There was such perfect joy and such a pure love in that place that I knew Jesus had entered the room, through His Holy Spirit. I didn't see Him—although some people had visions that night of a bright white light with a rainbow-hued glow—but I felt Him. I knew beyond any doubt that Jesus was there. Soon the preacher was sobbing and unable to preach.

Then it happened.

The sermon wasn't over. No altar call was made. But it happened anyway: Blind people spontaneously stood and began to declare that they could see! Shouts of joy rose throughout the church.

The prayer team got up and began to pray for anyone and everyone who wanted prayer.

The joy and love was so real in the church that people's faces seemed to glow. No national or cultural barriers, language differences, socioeconomic disparity, or anything else separated the people in the room from each other spiritually and emotionally.

Christ's love was so pure, so perfect, and so real that none of those things mattered. There was a unity of the Spirit like I had never known.

Besides the people who had never seen before receiving their eyesight, several who had been deaf began to hear, and the mute spoke. The unmistakable, perfect presence of Jesus brought sight to eyes and hearing to ears and a cleansing to hearts that night.

I prayed with many people, including the most beautiful man I'd ever seen. He was an older gentleman who, I surmised, was a leader in the deaf congregation and was a deaf mute. His only concern seemed to be that others receive prayer first.

When I say that he was beautiful, it is because I saw the reflection of God's love shining through him. I couldn't sign and I couldn't speak Spanish, but I could pray in a language that God understood.

We prayed and prayed, and soon he began to form the only Spanish words that I could shout into his ears, "Gloria a Dios!"

It was truly glorious. The joy on his face as he began to hear and speak was beyond human description. Our whole team prayed late into the night as the glorious presence of Jesus remained in the room. His presence brought the miracles of salvation to the lost, a cleansing to the hearts of those in the church, sight to the blind, hearing to the ears of the deaf, and words to the tongues of the mute.

The scene reminded me of the prophecy found in Isaiah 35:5–6 (NKJV):

> Then the eyes of the blind shall be opened, and the ears of the deaf shall be unstopped. Then the lame shall leap like a deer, and the tongue of the dumb sing. For waters shall burst forth in the wilderness, and streams in the desert.

While I was in the midst of Jesus' glorious presence that night, I remembered the vision I'd seen years earlier—of the women on the beach. As I looked around the room at the beautiful brown-skinned, black-haired women scattered throughout the congregation in this island nation, I knew that God fulfills His promises, no matter how long it takes.

How about you? Is there an unfulfilled vision in your heart? Know that God's timing is perfect, and He will do what He promised.

A Bible for a Thief

GRACE MARK

I longed for my husband to return to us, but he never would again.

On the second evening of our spring trip to Florida, I leaned against the headboard of the queen-sized bed. My preschool son and daughter nestled under each of my arms, listening as I read aloud Randy Alcorn's book *Heaven*. We all longed to know about their father's new home.

When I turned off the lights, the kids' breathing quieted into an even rhythm. Lying between them, I stared past the windows at the glowing moon, listening to the waves of Clearwater Beach. My chest ached as if its muscles pulled north, south, east, and west.

Two months earlier, in February, my young husband, Andrew, had died.

When my good friend Melissa and I had planned to leave Minnesota and take our kids on vacation, I assumed Florida could not bring any painful memories, since Andrew and I had never visited there together.

Instead, memories flew at us.

As we sat in the blue seats of the airplane on the way to Florida, my four-year-old's eyes lowered. The corners of his mouth dropped. "I just feel so sad because I don't have my papa."

The destination didn't matter. We were sitting in the blue seats without Andrew.

When we exited the airport, something familiar nagged at me. How could the palm trees remind me of Los Angeles, when Florida is humid and Los Angeles is dry desert? How could it remind me of falling in love with Andrew at always sunny and beautiful UCLA? Or remind me of the fact that we not only both studied there, but had both grown up in New Jersey? Six years earlier, Andrew had said that we could fly home to the East Coast together on our breaks. He said if we ran out of words on the five-hour flight, we could just kiss.

When Melissa, the kids, and I arrived at the vacation condo, we settled into our rooms. Admiring the beach out the window, however, reminded me of how Andrew loved such views.

Suddenly every memory of every vacation with Andrew flew at me. The images merged into a single memory, as if they had all happened in Florida, forcing me to think through them, to separate my knotted spaghetti thoughts. The time we accompanied him on a business trip to Coeur d'Alene, Idaho, and stayed in a hotel overlooking a sparkling azure lake when Gracie was a baby and A.J. a toddler. This melded into the memory when just he and I stayed in a hotel beside the Pacific Ocean in Canada after he recovered from his first time through radiation and chemo.

With those thoughts squeezing my heart, I fell asleep.

The next morning, our third day of vacation, I couldn't find my purse in the condo. Then I remembered. The night before, distracted by showering the sand off my children's feet, I'd left my purse beside the outdoor shower.

After checking the shower, the pool, and all possible lost and founds, I had to admit that someone had taken advantage of the opportunity and stolen my purse.

My purse contained my license and my cell phone. In less than two days, I needed my license to fly back to Minnesota. And my cell phone contained a voicemail that I had saved for over a year—one of the last recordings of Andrew's precious voice telling me that our son, A.J., had just told Andrew that he wanted to pray that Jesus would save him.

A month after that recording, Andrew had been diagnosed, and the tongue cancer quickly stole his beautiful voice.

Uncertain of what to do, Melissa and I proceeded with our beach plans. As the kids built sand castles, I walked nearby, the sand massaging my toes. Breathing in the salty air, I tried to relax my tight neck and shoulders. The sun glimmered like diamonds on the emerald water.

"What is the beauty in my situation, Lord? How could this be for my good and for your glory?"

Maybe you'll get to talk to someone about Jesus because of this.

An hour later, alone in the condo and using Melissa's red Blackberry, I called my sister.

"Lord," she prayed, "please give the thieves a change of heart and return Grace's purse."

It had never occurred to me to pray for that.

Next, I called Verizon. They said if I switched my plan to a new cell phone, my voicemail would be deleted. The only way to get my voicemail back was to get my phone back.

I called my cell phone for what seemed the twentieth time that day. It rang, but no one answered. And then I wondered why it never went straight to voicemail. For some reason, the thief had not shut my cell phone off. Also, in spite of missing its nightly charging, my phone's battery persisted.

I talked with my in-laws. They instructed me to contact countless places: "Call the airlines. Call the DMV. You need to postpone your flight at least a week so you can get a new license."

As I hung up, the sour taste of panic seeped into my mouth. I felt so overwhelmed.

Past the windows, the sea sparkled. Only a thin veil lay between Andrew and me. If only I could reach beyond it and just touch him.

"Lord!" I cried out. "You promise you are a Husband to the husbandless! And you *know* that this would never have happened if my husband had not died! You know that I never lost my purse before he died. Please! This situation is too big for me. But this is so easy for you. *Please!* I need my wallet and my cell phone back!"

Suddenly, a gentle ringing—Melissa's phone. On its gray screen, it said, "Grace calling."

My cell phone was calling me back!

"Pleeease," I answered. "My husband just died and I'm *really* having a hard time." My voice squeaked like a squirrel's last desperate breaths after being run over. "Pleeease, I just need my license and my cell phone back. Pleeease."

I heard a male voice: "Sure, we'll return your stuff," as if it were a normal request.

But as we talked a bit, underneath the nonchalance, I heard a real human being. The Holy Spirit gave me a longing to hand him something that shared about Jesus. But I had no tracts with me. *Lord, please provide something I can give them.*

I asked him to meet me at the condo's security guard booth.

Beside the security guard booth, a blond teenage boy leaned his back against a car. Inside, a dark-haired teenage boy sat in the driver's seat, and a very pregnant girl sat in the passenger seat.

Scrawny, I thought of the boys. *They're no threat.*

The dark-haired one explained to the security guard, "We were with a large group, jumped the fence, and swam in the pool. And then this guy saw the purse and took it. Someone's friend. We don't even know him. We knew it was wrong, so we're returning the purse."

While the security guard continued grilling the dark-haired one, I approached the blond kid. He handed me my wallet and cell phone.

"Thank you *so so* much for coming back here and returning it. I don't know *what* I would have done if you hadn't."

The blond boy lowered his chin, a shadow of guilt in his eyes.

"I wanted to give you this." I handed him Andrew's three-dollar pew Bible he'd bought the previous year. He had written his name, "Andrew Mark," in his engineer's handwriting—all caps in thick black ink on the back cover.

The young man's chin lowered more, the guilt expanding in his eyes.

"My husband died two months ago of cancer at twenty-seven years old. If you had known him ten years ago, you probably would have been friends with him."

And now his chin dropped so low, it nearly touched his chest. Guilt flooded his eyes.

"Please read the book of John."

He nodded.

They left and I returned to the condo. But as I boiled pasta at the stove with Melissa, the Holy Spirit caused my heart to long to share Jesus with those boys, who were probably the real thieves. *Lord, please provide a way for me to talk to them.*

The landline on the wall rang. When I answered, the security guard said, "The boys have returned. They want to speak to you."

Thank you, Lord!

At the security gate, the two boys stood outside their car. The pregnant girl was gone. The guilty-looking blond boy held Andrew's black pew Bible.

The dark-haired one said, "We can't accept this."

"Andrew would want you to have it," I insisted. "Before he became a Christian and before I met him, he did all kinds of reckless things. And if you knew him, he would understand you and would want you to know his Savior."

"We're the ones who stole your purse!" Blondie admitted.

"I know." Nothing anyone could do to me, though, no matter how awful that day was, could compare to what I did to Jesus on the cross, nailing Him there daily with each of my sins. I shrugged. "I forgive you."

"*You do?*" The blond one stared at me wide-eyed, his mouth hanging open. "Every lie we told felt like a knife stab."

It was as if the Lord had pursued them like an angry Husband, the Protector of His wife—only this Husband was omnipresent and could follow them in their car and could influence their consciences.

"And so we just *had* to return your stuff to you."

My sister, Gayle, whom I had called earlier, had specifically prayed that the purse thieves would have a change of heart. And that is what happened.

For the next hour, they let me share the Gospel.

I gave them my email address, and later the blond one emailed me several times thanking me profusely. I looked up churches in his area and he went a couple of times. I prayed God would surround him with other Christians. Eventually, he became a professional boxer. His coach was a Christian, took him to church, and met with him weekly to teach him how to study the Bible. As the years went by, at least once a year, Blondie would email and update me on his life.

One summer, Blondie lived in New Jersey. Though he did not attend my old church there, he happened to meet my pastor's son—they boxed at the same gym. The Lord had answered my prayer that God would surround Blondie with Christians.

When I returned from Florida to Minnesota, I talked to a friend from church who was a Minneapolis police officer. He said, "When someone gets her purse stolen, it never gets returned. This is completely unheard of!"

The Lord also made my cell phone last without its essential nightly re-charge. If my phone had run out of battery, the teenagers never would have been able to call me back on Melissa's cell phone.

Twice I cried out to God, and the phone rang with the thieves on the other side. There is no other explanation except that God himself truly answers prayers. He had done the impossible—thieves had a change of heart and returned their plunder.

That first year after my husband died, it was as if I saw God with my own eyes, experiencing His faithfulness over and over. And this miracle was one of the inarguable experiences in which God proved His promise that He truly is a Husband to the husbandless.

Who Really Took the Test?

KAREN R. HESSEN

"Karen, report to the counseling office." My homeroom teacher handed me the call slip.

I walked across the school grounds dedicated in 1922, past the vine-covered three-story buildings. The campus, resembling an Ivy League college, was tucked away on a little hilltop in Southern California. On this breezy fall day, the gray quarry stone buildings were especially lovely against the blue autumn sky.

Meeting with Mr. Wyatt, my high school counselor, had become a weekly experience since the beginning of my senior year at Grossmont High. The topic was always the same. "What have you decided to do with your life?"

"I really haven't decided yet," was always my answer.

At age five, I had accepted Christ as my personal Savior, was baptized, and followed Him as fervently as a child can.

At summer camp in fifth grade, I dedicated my life to Christian service.

Now a high school senior, I could not choose a career without His direction. I had considered teaching, missions, social work, and many other options. I had not felt the Holy Spirit blessing any of these possibilities.

It was time to prepare for my future. What was God's plan for me?

At home that afternoon, I told Mother I would be spending the evening in my room. I wanted to take extra time in prayer seeking God's direction for my life.

At my bedside I prayed until I had no more words. While I slept, God spoke.

"Mother! Daddy! I know what I'm supposed to do. I'm going to be a nurse."

Mother and Daddy were still sleeping when I barged into their room. They were too surprised to say much, but Mother, knowing my prayer vigil, supported my decision.

At school, I parked my copper-colored '56 Chevy coupe in the senior parking lot. I hurried into Mr. Wyatt's office, this time without waiting for him to summon me but with plenty of excitement and peace of mind.

"Mr. Wyatt, I need a brochure and an application for admission to Grossmont Vocational School of Nursing," I blurted out.

"I must advise you, Karen, you have no aptitude for nursing. You are gifted in languages. They are your best bet," he said impatiently.

"I am sure about this, Mr. Wyatt. I already committed my life to Christian service. I've been waiting for God's guidance before choosing a direction for my life. I've prayed about this, and I know it's what He wants me to do."

Mr. Wyatt thumbed through the vertical files behind his desk and handed me the information I requested. "I must tell you this is a mistake, but it is your mistake to make."

I found the school's phone number in the brochure.

"Hello. My name is Karen Brown. I want to apply for admission to your school and make arrangements to take the entrance exams," I said to the person who answered the phone.

"How old are you?"

"I will be seventeen next week."

"Are you still in high school?"

"Yes. I graduate in June."

"We will gladly accept your application, but you should not take the entrance exams until after you graduate. You will not pass."

"I really want to test as soon as possible."

"I cannot refuse to let you test, but I strongly urge you to wait. You will not pass. When you fail you will not be allowed to retest. Do you understand?"

"Yes, I do. I want to test."

"Then you can test as soon as you turn seventeen. When will that be?"

"Next Thursday is my birthday."

"We will be giving the test next Friday. It takes seven hours. Be here at 8:00 a.m. Bring your completed application and a twenty-five-dollar testing fee. Everything else you need to know is explained in the school's brochure. I hope you will reconsider and postpone your testing until next summer. Call me if you change your mind."

I spent a good deal of time between that phone call and the following Friday in prayer. When the test date arrived I was "prayed up." Armed with the completed application and Daddy's check for twenty-five dollars, I signed in at the exam site.

"Miss Brown?"

"Yes."

"May I see you, please?"

The immaculate woman in the nurse's uniform was Catherine Forbes, RN, the director of nursing. "It is in your best interest to test next summer, after you graduate." I recognized her voice as the person who had taken my call a week earlier.

"I am prepared to take the test today," I answered.

"You do understand that you will not be allowed to retest?" Mrs. Forbes asked.

"I do."

The exam room contained nineteen other people plus Mrs. Forbes. The long, narrow room was apparently used as a classroom for the nursing program. Anatomy charts hung on the walls. A skeleton dangled from a stainless steel frame at the head of the class. The chalk trays were filled with fine yellow dust. The eighteen women and one man were all older than me. The youngest was at least twice my age. The exam was to be given in several thirty- to ninety-minute segments: math, English, logic, problem solving, and so on. Seats were assigned to prevent cheating.

In spite of being "prayed up," I prayed again, asking Jesus to give me peace, before opening my test booklet.

I read the first question. Then I really prayed. If it was truly God's will for me to become a nurse, and I believed it was, then He was going to have to send someone to answer these questions. They were way too difficult for me. I did not understand the questions. How would I ever select the correct answers from the choices provided?

There were words in the first question I did not recognize. This was the math section. I had never seen some of this terminology. I gave my number two pencil and answer grid sheet to God.

I did not stress over my performance on the exam. Jesus' presence in my life gave me the confidence to know He was in control. Using my hand to guide His pencil, Jesus spent the next seven hours filling in bubbles on His answer pages.

At the end of each test section, I noticed Mrs. Forbes set my answer grid to her left. All the other applicants' sheets were stacked in a pile. I could not be certain, but it appeared that she was correcting my exam immediately after I completed each section.

Three-thirty—over at last!

"Miss Brown, may I see you, please? I was so certain you would not pass that I have been scoring your test as you handed in each section. I must tell you, you have passed each section. In fact, you passed each section at the level of someone with a PhD, except for the math section. That one you passed at the level of a master's degree. We will be pleased to have you in our school. Have your counselor send your transcripts as soon as possible."

A master's degree, indeed, I thought, knowing God had taken the test in my place and started me on the Master Plan for my life. *Not today, Jesus, but someday I'll tell Mrs. Forbes who really took the test.*

The Road to Jesus

DANA SCOTT

As I stepped down from the school bus, I wanted to go anyplace but home. I dreaded walking into that rental house.

My eyes scanned the March skies. The angry, threatening clouds matched the mood and dark thoughts churning nonstop through my thirteen-year-old mind.

I knew I needed to hurry to make it the half mile home before the rains came. But my feet dragged as I zigzagged back and forth to avoid the water-filled potholes on the muddy, graveled road.

Why should I be in a rush to open that door? It was worse being in that house than in any storm.

Every day we kids faced the same anger and turmoil. Our parents had waged constant war with each other since our family had moved to the Pacific Northwest three months earlier. My six younger brothers and sisters and I lived in constant fear of saying or doing anything that might set them off on another barrage of shouting, name calling, and cursing.

Our mom needed security, but our dad had no job. They had spent the last of their savings on the rent. Our only food for the past month had been hundred-pound sacks of potatoes and parsnips. I could not stand one more parsnip. No matter how hard I tried to keep them down, they made me gag.

I was the new kid at school. My first seven years of school had been spent in the sheltered setting of a one-room schoolhouse in rural Minnesota. We had one teacher who taught a total of sixteen students in all eight grades. Now I had to deal with a city junior high school with four hundred kids.

To say I was overwhelmed is a gross understatement. How could I ever fit in? I was the outsider, a misfit, and all the kids knew it. In those early teen years, it was so important to dress, talk, and act like your classmates. But my clothing from the farm and my clipped Minnesota brogue set me apart from them.

To get a free lunch, my mom had signed me up to be cafeteria clean-up help. Everybody knew you couldn't afford to buy a lunch if you did clean-up duty. Day after day I felt more isolated and incapable of speaking to anyone, especially to my parents. They had their own problems. I was alone.

My pace slowed even more as I dreaded the moment I would have to open the front door of the place we now called home.

To this day I have no idea why my feet suddenly stopped, unable to take another step, as though rooted to the road. Nor have I ever known why these words came from my lips: "Jesus, O Jesus, why am I going through all of this? I just can't take it anymore."

During our growing-up years, we kids never saw a Bible in our home, and we were not a churchgoing family. We did not say grace at meals or ever pray, not even when one of my brothers was hospitalized and critically ill. The only time we heard God's name was in moments of anger.

But during the summer of my tenth year, for a brief time, a dear lady named Hazel had driven five miles from town to our farm to take us older children to Sunday school. She had heard about our large family from our schoolteacher. Our mother had agreed, so Hazel picked us up and drove us to church three or four times. But that stopped when our father found out and decided he didn't trust her driving.

My best memory of our few hours in that church classroom was finding out I had a soul. As we stood on a sheet of black paper, our teacher traced the outline of our foot and we cut it out. Then she told us that without Jesus, our souls were black with sin. Sadly, the lesson stopped there. No call was given to ask Jesus into our hearts. But apparently I'd heard the truth that Jesus loved me.

As I stood in the middle of the road, in the space of a heartbeat, the sun's rays illuminated a straight path through the dark clouds. The light shone directly on me, warming me on the inside, and then spreading throughout the rest of my body.

My eyes watered as I tried to take in the road before me. It glittered as though strewn with diamonds; the roadside grass and trees shined as though painted with crystals. Then a sweet and gentle voice spoke to my mind and my heart, saying, "I am making you strong."

I spun around looking for the person who spoke. No one was there. Again, the voice said, "I am making you strong."

I have no idea how long I stood there. It seemed almost forever, because time had no meaning as my heart sang. I wanted to stay in that sweet and loving presence forever. He did not speak again, but His words gave hope to my heart. I felt so humbled and in awe He cared so much that He would speak to me. His words gave me the courage to face the challenges of those dark days of adolescence and feel encouragement for better times to come.

I don't believe I fully valued and appreciated His words to me until thirteen years later. With no warning, my world crashed. I had been married for nearly seven years to the man I thought was to be my life and my love forever. The only warning I had was that he had stopped going to church soon after our wedding vows were spoken.

Our goals included my supporting him so he could focus on earning his college degree. This I did for three years. After college, he started his own fence construction company, and we decided the time was right to begin our family. When our son was two and a half and our little daughter had just celebrated her first birthday, my husband began to drink and not come home at night.

I had no idea how to deal with this. It was so out of character for him. He'd never touched alcohol during the first five years of our marriage.

He changed before my eyes from a tender, loving husband and father into an angry, brooding man. When I tried to get him to talk to me, he'd leave, slam the door, jump in the car, and spin gravel out the driveway. Three months later, on another blustery March day, he came home early one morning.

"I don't want to be married anymore. I don't want to be a father," he announced. "I'm not paying the rent on this house anymore. You and the kids have to be out. The rent is paid for only five more days. And I'm leaving."

He slapped down a ten-dollar bill, saying, "This is all I have and I bought you a car. Here's the keys. It's out front."

He tossed the keys on the kitchen table, turned, and left without even a good-bye to his children.

For the next few days, I could do nothing but bawl and try to care for and feed these two little ones. The physical pain was horrible.

"Yes," I said to myself, "a person can die from a broken heart."

Mine was ripped in two. He had taken half of it out that door with him.

By the middle of the third night of no sleep, and when we had only two more days with a roof over our heads, Jesus gently began to remind me of His words to me on that March day so many years before: "I am making you strong."

Haltingly, I began to talk to Him. "Yes, Lord Jesus, I know you are here with me."

Before I knew it, everything came pouring out to Him—my brokenness, my grief, and my worries about providing for these precious children with no job and only ten dollars.

Then I slept.

After my first night's sleep in three days, I awoke and was able to think clearly. These two sweet children and their well-being had to be my first priority. Even though my husband's folks lived close by and would gladly help us, I simply could not break their hearts by telling them what their son had become, so I decided I had to leave without telling them.

After I'd spent that night with Jesus' reminder of His making me strong, it seemed as though He was the One making the decisions and taking action. I phoned my sister who lived two hours away in a large city where jobs would be more plentiful than in our college town.

She kindly invited us into her home until I could find work. She also knew of a good child care provider.

Next I dismantled our children's beds and loaded the panels and mattresses into the back of the station wagon my husband had bought us. They just barely fit.

"Oh, thank you, Jesus," I whispered.

I packed bedding, clothes, photos, and as many kitchen items as that wagon could hold. It was loaded to the ceiling with only enough space left for us to sit.

We made the drive to my sister's only by Jesus' provision and protection. For as we drove the freeway on that dark and rainy March night, a short in the electrical system on that old wagon burned up all the wiring. We managed the last fifty miles with no lights, no heat, and no windshield wipers. But that car's motor kept running and we made it safely. Again, I thanked Jesus.

Within a week's time, He gave me a job and a rental house to share with another single mom, who was raising three boys. Two years later, I married a man who was more than willing to be a husband and "Daddy" to our ready-made family.

For ten years we had no word from the children's father. We hadn't even known where he was when the phone rang one day and he asked to see "his kids." After a family discussion, all four of us agreed that meeting him was the right thing to do.

Naturally, the children were curious about this man they knew was their birth father but didn't remember anything about. By this time, both were middle school students.

The meeting went well and I could tell that the children had adjusted well to this new facet of life. They chose to call him by his first name instead of giving a fatherly title to him.

Today, when more of my earthly years are behind me, I'm struck by just how extraordinary my experience of meeting Jesus was. I can never thank Him enough or praise Him enough for that stormy day when He called me out. Without Him I never could have survived the storms that have come my way. His strength and His love enabled me to be strong enough to fully forgive and to see my first husband as He sees him—through eyes of mercy.

May you also lean into our Lord's strength and may He shine through you today as you face your own challenges of life.

A Walk of a Lifetime

CONNIE SORRELL

D on't shut the door," my son Rodney said from his reclining motor lift bed that hospice had supplied.

I slipped through the doorway into the dark room. A square of moonlight spotlighted the recliner by the open window, giving enough light for me to see as I walked between the recliner and the bed. I reached for Rodney's right hand that used to be calloused from fixing truck tires; it was moist and soft.

"How are you tonight?" I whispered, not wanting to wake up my father-in-law, who was sleeping on a single bed to Rodney's left side.

"Oh, all right," he replied. His voice sounded flat and tired. I glanced at the digital clock on the night table by his bed.

"It's midnight," I said, squeezing his hand. "You should be sleeping."

He turned his face toward the open door. I stepped closer and ruffled his wavy sandy brown hair with my fingers. His long eyelashes blinked over his big brown eyes.

"Isn't the night lovely?" he asked. "The nature God made is pretty. When He heals me of this cancer, I'm gonna walk all over this earth and tell about His glory."

His strong statement put a lump in my throat, so I silently followed his gaze outside, where the dark green cedar trees swayed to the rhythm of gentle breezes. The crickets and locusts played a concert in the trimmed carpet of grass. The blacktop drive I had driven over curved through the lawn to the church's family units. These are twelve family motel rooms with doors opening to the outside, six toward the east and six toward the west. Room seven toward the west was a quiet haven where Rodney could rest away from our busy house.

From this doorway we had a clear view of the brown metal two-story schoolhouse where seven of our children learned academics and respect for God and His Word. Rodney was number four of ours to graduate, with two brothers graduating later and a younger sister still learning there.

When it was church time, we went to the red and brown brick chapel east of the school. I shut my damp eyes and saw Rodney as a baby, toddler, boy, and then a young man coming through the chapel doors. I saw his grin as he greeted people.

Oh, Lord, we need a U-turn! I prayed. *Deliver him from this cancer NOW! Please! For his twenty-fifth birthday—please!*

As I continued to pray, I felt my muscles relax.

Focus on the peace of this moment, the Lord said to me. *Rodney needs to feel your confidence in me. Encourage his strength and trust in me.*

By the grace of God, I was able to obey. After a few more whispered words, I succumbed to sleep in the recliner.

The summer sunshine roused me from my rest. I heard my husband's arrival and his father's departure at nine o'clock.

"Good morning, son!" Dwane greeted Rodney. "You look cheery this morning. Are you ready for the physical therapist?"

Rodney flashed his sunny smile that had won him friends in Germany, Canada, Honduras, and in many states, especially in the southern states where he had driven a dump truck with loads of debris from the homes damaged by Hurricane Katrina.

"You know I like visitors," he replied to his dad. He placed his arms on the pillows above his head. "I'll talk to you later. Here comes Sheri."

Knock-knock! Sheri opened the door. "Hello! How is my favorite client?"

"Ready to go, if you are!" responded Rodney with a twinkle in his big brown eyes.

Sheri helped Rodney through various exercises. We watched Rodney push buttons on his motor lift bed with the same enthusiasm he had when a couple of years ago he had bought a 4x4 Chevy truck with a suspension lift. As his truck idled in our driveway, Rodney had pushed buttons and pulled levers to show his dad and three brothers all the bells and whistles on what I called a "monster truck."

He should be driving that truck instead of pushing buttons on a hospital bed, I thought. *Oh, Lord, when are you going to come to his rescue?*

Sheri's voice broke into my thoughts.

"You are so enthusiastic!" she exclaimed as she patted Rodney's arm. "I could stay here all day and work with you just for that smile, but I have more clients to see."

After Sheri's cheery good-bye, Rodney turned his face toward us. "Come over by me," he said. "Let me tell you who came to visit me early this morning."

"Oh?" I questioned.

Rodney's eyes sparkled as he said, "Dad, Mom, Jesus visited me this morning! I was praying and looking out the door. Mom, you were sleeping and so was Grandpa when this bright light filled the room. Then Jesus came in. I got out of bed and walked to Him. He took me into His arms and gave me a big hug. I will never forget that hug. It was so warm and tight. I leaned my head on His shoulder, and Jesus said, 'Rodney, you are going to be okay. You are resting in my arms. I am taking care of you.'

"I relaxed. I felt so relieved, so full of warm courage. Then Jesus left and I went into a deep sleep. I woke up after a while and was praying when that same warm, bright light filled this room again. It seemed to be in me and all around me, and I knew Jesus was in that light again."

I patted his face and ran my fingers through his hair. His dad put his arm around Rodney's thin shoulders. Tears streamed down our faces.

"Don't cry." His voice was cheery. "Jesus is taking care of me. I believe I will be walking soon. I am in a win-win situation with Jesus. He said I am going to be okay, so don't cry."

We had to dry our tears for his sake. In spite of the pain in his deteriorating body, his soul was full of joy.

This happiness spilled over to the ambulance crew as Rodney was transported to the hospital that afternoon. He shared the visit from Jesus with doctors, nurses, chaplains, the cleaning lady—all the many visitors he had through the ten days in ICU. When he was on the ventilator, he texted messages of "Look up to Jesus," "Meet me up there," and "I'm going home soon" to many friends.

On Sunday morning, June 28, on his twenty-fifth birthday, Rodney asked the doctors to take off the ventilator so he could talk with family and see the hundred birthday cards he had received. They told him if they took it off, his body would live only a few hours.

As soon as he could talk again, Rodney rasped encouragement to us. His youngest sister, Darlene, could not bear to see her brother so sick. She stayed in the lounge with praying friends.

Lyndall and Kevin, Rodney's brothers, went back and forth between Rodney's room and the lounge as they tried to get Gerald, their youngest brother, home from Marine duty. Susan and Jennifer, Rodney's sisters, read cards to him when he had to catch a breath from talking. His brothers- and sisters-in-law and his four grandparents came into the room to quietly hear Rodney's testimony.

Rodney wanted so much to see and talk to Gerald, but his strength began to fade as the sun went down. Softly we sang songs about heaven, Jesus, and the love of God. Rodney's courageous walk in the light and into the arms of Jesus gave us the strength to release him.

Through tears of sorrow and of joy, we told Gerald about Rodney's vision, and as we continue to tell it, others have gained courage to walk with Jesus into the light of heaven.

The Broken Vessel
Jesus Chose

KRISTINA LANDRUM
AS TOLD TO DONNA SCALES

For an hour I'd poured out the story of my life to my new friend, my Christian mentor. When I finished talking, she didn't say anything for a long time. Then she blurted, "After all you'd been through, why on earth did you choose Jesus? Quite honestly, I would think you'd be mad at God."

As I thought about her question, a smile seemed to spread from my toes all the way to my face, and, with complete conviction, I announced, "Jesus protected me for His purpose! He saved me from all that chaos so I could give others hope."

Since I came into this world, my life has been extremely rough, and for most of it I've been angry with God. Right now I'm an inmate at the Oregon Women's Correctional Facility—with a long sentence for manslaughter.

I never knew my biological father. My mom was an alcoholic and cocaine addict. In my whole life I never saw her clean or sober. In fact, she died from her addiction.

When I was nine I was sent to live with my aunt and uncle. At first I was excited because I thought I'd finally be a part of a family—something I'd longed for. Then my uncle sexually abused me for two long, painful, confusing years.

My friend wanted to know more. She asked, "Have you ever sensed the presence of God along the agonizing path that has been your life?"

I told her about an incident from my childhood that has remained vivid in my memory.

I've always been afraid of the dark. When I was still living with my mother, I was scared of the closet at the foot of my bed. Each night before I went to bed I'd make sure the door was firmly latched.

One night I was awakened by a quiet, gentle voice calling my name. I looked around, but nobody was there. I heard the call a second and then a third time. I finally got out of bed and went to my mother's room—she was asleep. Coming back into my room, I was scared spitless to see that the closet door was unlatched. I tiptoed to the door and opened it.

"Please don't hurt me!" I begged.

Whoever was there said He wouldn't hurt me. A comforting presence filled me, and we had a conversation. He told me He knew all about me, that He loved me, and, despite what was happening in my life, He was watching over me. I then went back to bed and slept soundly. Jesus had come to help me.

"And was there any Christian influence in your life?" my friend asked.

"There was only one—my grandmother. Grama prayed for me for forty years. She's been the only constant in my life. She visits me in prison every month."

Nobody led me to Jesus. I guess you could say He came and got me—at His perfect time. He didn't stop me from making poor choices for many years, like taking and selling drugs, selling my body, and being convicted of manslaughter. He allowed me to endure the consequences of every choice I made.

When I could take no more, He intervened.

On December 14, 2009, a policeman had his gun trained on my back and hollered, "Stop or I'll shoot!"

Following a high-speed chase, I'd jumped out of my car and was trying to escape. Despite the policeman's command, I had every intention of running. Then came a more compelling command—which I believe was directly from Jesus himself—"No, stop!"

The words seemed almost audible.

I tried to run, but my feet felt superglued to the ground, like something was holding me to that spot. The hands of Jesus?

I made another attempt to run, but my legs simply would not move.

I was taken to the justice center, interrogated, booked into custody, and put in a cell. Near my bed I noticed there was a book published by a prison ministry. It said the author had been in prison, so I decided to read some of it and was immediately captured by Jeremiah 29:11: "'For I know the plans I have for you,' declares the Lord, 'plans to prosper you and not to harm you, plans to give you hope and a future.'"

Oh, how I wanted that to be true for me!

I slid off the bed onto my knees and bawled. I poured out every sin I'd ever committed and begged God to forgive me. I asked Jesus to come into my life . . . and I've never looked back!

Since I've been in prison, I've voluntarily taken classes that required me to identify things I've done wrong. In fact, my list filled seven pages—very humbling and humiliating. I have taken responsibility for my past actions—no more blaming others, no more excuses, only accountability.

When Jesus came into my heart, my whole perspective on life shifted. Being accountable brought freedom from all the baggage I'd carried for so long. I'd been living as a slave to those memories and to the pain. Jesus not only brought me spiritual freedom, but mental freedom as well.

I'm that broken vessel He chose to use! I study my Bible daily and ask God to help me be a light to the other women within the prison. He's helped me draw on skills that were hidden inside for so long and inspired me to write a proposal for a mentoring program here at the prison. The corrections officials responded enthusiastically to my proposal and have just recently approved it.

In one of my early Bible study groups, the leader suggested that I replace the word *Israel* with my name in Old Testament promises, claiming them for myself. The following is my all-time favorite, taken from Isaiah 43:1–5 (NKJV):

> Thus says the Lord, who created you, O Kristina, and He who formed you: "Fear not, for I have redeemed you; I have called you by your name; you are Mine. When you pass through the waters, I will be with you; and through the rivers, they shall not overflow you. When you walk through the fire, you shall not be burned, nor shall the flame scorch you. For I am the Lord your God, the Holy One of Kristina, your Savior. . . . Fear not, for I am with you."

The new perspective that I have today makes me realize that my grandmother wasn't the only constant all those years. Jesus has been there, too, and He continues to support and strengthen me for the challenges of prison life.

Jesus on the Cross

PATRICIA ANNE ELFORD

As we sang familiar hymns in the evening service, my throat ached. Tears leaked off my chin onto the hymnal I shared with the motherly looking stranger beside me.

Drip. Drip.

It was a mistake to come to worship in the church where Donald and I were married! Who knew that being in this sanctuary would trigger my tears? What must the woman sharing our soggy hymnbook think of me?

As the service ended, the stranger, whom I learned was named Ruth, asked, "Is something wrong?"

"I've just moved away from my abusive husband. We got married here. Worshiping where our wedding took place overwhelmed me."

"I'd like you to join us at our home Bible study and prayer group on Wednesday."

What? Go to church in the morning? Go to church in the evening? Then go to a mid-week Bible study? That's a bit much!
But I was lonely.

At the first meeting, they took turns praying aloud. Although I'd grown up in the church, besides sharing the Lord's Prayer, I'd never prayed aloud with others. Pressure built inside my chest. The praying did not go around the circle; rather, people seemed to erupt spontaneously a moment or two after another person's brief prayer finished. The pressure eased.

During the study I felt welcomed and listened attentively. For the next study, however, a woman brought her husband, a man who was not completely committed to Christ, but was testing the waters.

How handsome and pleasant he is. . . . Good grief. I didn't even hear what the leader was saying! What's wrong with me? I'm at a Bible study and I'm focusing on another person's husband, the only other unconvinced Christian here! How I wish I could believe as deeply as the rest of them do!

I continued to participate in the prayer and study group; I don't even remember if that woman's husband came back. I continued to teach school, throwing myself into the work I loved. I attended worship services. Each night in my sparsely furnished apartment, even though I was pregnant with my abusive husband's baby, I knelt to pray for guidance and strength.

One night, as I knelt there praying in the semi-darkness, something happened. I heard nothing, but as I looked up from my hands to a point in front of me, higher than my head, I saw Jesus, on the cross. He looked so very real, in pain, bleeding. Though I'm intuitive, I'm not subject to hallucinations or visions. It never entered my head to *ask* for a vision. If I'd thought about it, I would have been *afraid* to think of such a thing happening up close and personal. I did not reach out to touch Jesus, but there was, and is, no doubt in my mind that Jesus had somehow manifested himself to me in this way.

For years I'd been known as a "good, honest girl," and, apart from a few slips, agreed with that appraisal. But now! Looking at Jesus Christ—suffering? First fearful, I was next overwhelmed by my part in His torture and death. I'd heard the words for years, but now, my part in it had become real. . . . *He* was real.

I don't know how long I wept and begged for forgiveness with my mind flooded and my heart pained by realizing the many ways I'd betrayed Christ for so long. Sorrow kept me praying and weeping until I became aware of being forgiven. Then the feeling was overwhelming gratitude and joy. I finally climbed into bed drained but reassured and comforted. I slept well.

The next morning I awoke lighthearted. I sang and practically skipped on the way to the bus to go to work. I felt as if Jesus were holding my hand. I couldn't stop smiling all day. I was forgiven! I *knew* I was.

That night I phoned Ruth, fearing she'd think me mad, but I was bubbling to tell her what had happened. Though she celebrated and prayed with me, Ruth didn't seem surprised.

They've probably all been praying for me since I dampened the hymn book.

That meeting with Jesus altered my perspective. I grew braver, ready to trust God to carry me through one unknown situation after another—in work, in relationships, in life plans, and through the birth of my precious son and a near-death scare I had with him.

As my trust deepened, I undergirded everything with prayer—morning, noon, and night.

I began to recognize coincidences as being God at work in my life.

I was active in a Christian group when I returned to classes at the university for more education. A speaker came to visit. He talked about a summer Christian outreach center that he and his wife, both younger than I, would be in charge of as house parents. After he spoke to our group, he took me aside.

"I feel that you're meant to be there," he said.

"Oh, I don't think so. I'm older than all of you. I have a toddler son and graduate in June. Then I'm headed to teach at a Christian school in a small town after the summer. Each person has to contribute to support the center you talked about. What could *I* do?"

I thought about it and prayed about it, but I still decided that this was where I should be the summer after graduation.

My main contributions would be editing and typing a graduate student's thesis as he completed it, and joining others in Christian witnessing at the beach and nearby streets.

Closer to graduation time, a former boss of mine from years earlier, Robert, suddenly contacted me. He was driving by the town I lived in when he stopped by the college campus, not knowing if I still lived there or not.

He found the right building, rang the buzzer, and announced himself through the intercom.

"Do you remember me?"

Of course I did—he had been my boss and had the most appealing, revealing blue eyes I'd ever seen.

"Come up for coffee and cookies."

On a normal Sunday afternoon, I would not have been there. I was at home *only because* I was washing up dishes after the extra Bible study our university group had held, hoping a particular couple would come. On any other Sunday at this time, I would have been walking around the campus and playing with my toddler son. Had Robert come even half an hour later, I would have been out rambling with my son. He'd have continued on his trip.

As we talked, I found out that his wife had left him and his children two years before, and he was no longer married. What had formerly been a work association turned into a warm friendship.

Robert and I knew almost immediately that something special was happening for us, but the fact that we were both Christians was not enough. What did *God* will for us as we were trying to live our now-broken lives faithfully?

The outreach center I'd committed myself to for the summer was a short drive from Robert's aunt's home. He and his girls would come stay with his aunt and visit me. We walked hand in hand on the beach and talked and got to know one another better.

We were married in Peterborough, England, in November. I cried through the vows, but stopped when it was time for communion.

As a newly married woman, I loved staying at home with the children for a few years. What fun that was! I was active in the church and led the Church Guides. After a few years, I returned to teach art, a favorite subject of mine, to grades seven and eight.

What I gained as a result of my newfound faith was not a perfect life, nor had I suddenly become a perfect person. Since that vision, though, I've been given inspiration and strength. I've been freed to gain successes and win opportunities and help others.

I've been carried in prayer through the miseries any woman might experience: attempted rape, the near-death of my newborn, a miscarriage, job loss, flooding, being the victim of malicious treatment, in need of food and financial assistance, and other experiences that could have destroyed our earthly lives. Did I mention my cancer, my husband's injuries, and our other physical health problems? My joy and peace are regularly renewed, but *not* because life holds no challenges.

Whenever I feel afraid, I don't whistle a happy tune, as an old musical recommends, though I may sing a hymn or chorus. I pray.

Sometimes I wonder, *Where can God be in this?*

Then I remember when Jesus visited me in the darkness of my barely furnished room, when all earthly happiness I'd experienced and expected had dissolved and my future was barren of hope.

No new visitation is needed—I remember, and fall on my knees once more. There is confession. There is gratitude. There is hope. Sometimes, there are tears.

A New Set of Lungs

LORETTA MILLER MEHL

The church my husband and I attended had several couples our age, including our friends Tom and Lorraine Bunner. We had known them for many years, and we found them to be dedicated Christians. Although Tom said very little about his faith, Lorraine spoke and wrote about her experience with the Lord.

Over several months, we noticed that Tom often coughed and appeared to have a difficult time breathing. When we asked about his health, he said he had been diagnosed with emphysema. The doctor had said there was no cure and that Tom's condition would only worsen.

The doctor also urged Tom to find another line of work, but that presented a huge problem: Tom had always only worked with plaster and cement, and he had no other training or skills. (He later learned that some mixtures he had worked with included asbestos.)

He knew he needed to change his type of work, but he had been hired by Los Angeles County and was reluctant to leave a secure position with a good salary.

As Tom's problems escalated, he was placed on our prayer lists. Many people who suffered serious health problems at that time discussed the miracles occurring at healing services held by Kathryn Kuhlman, an evangelist and faith healer, in a large Los Angeles auditorium.

Although my husband and I did not seek help, we attended one of these services and were amazed at those who appeared to be immediately healed when the healer's hands were laid upon them.

We were pleased that before the service began, the woman explained that God used her hands and prayers for those who asked to be healed. She emphasized the fact that she gave all the glory to God, who did the healing.

"I cannot heal anyone," she admitted.

As she placed hands on an individual, some people fell backward on the stage, where strong arms stood ready to catch them and prevent injury.

As the news of the miracles spread, Tom and Lorraine discussed the possibility of Tom attending a meeting to ask for healing. Although he was a young man and sought help from his doctors, Tom's breathing difficulty had increased, and he had bouts of difficult coughing. Nothing the doctors prescribed appeared to help. His doctors continued to urge him to immediately change his line of work, but he reminded the doctors he was not trained to do anything else and he needed the work to support his young children and wife.

As Tom's health continued to decline, Lorraine and Tom decided to attend a Kathryn Kuhlman service. However, when they arrived at the auditorium, the place was so packed they could barely find seats in the back row.

When the invitation was given, Tom did not go to the stage for prayer; instead, he and his wife prayed from where they sat.

Tom did not feel any different when they left for home, and he remembers still having great difficulty breathing. Although he felt sick during the following week, he returned to his usual work.

Several days later, while driving home from his job, Tom started coughing and became so nauseated he had to pull over to the side of the road. He barely had time to exit his truck before a black, offensive substance spewed from his mouth repeatedly.

"I had no doubt I had been completely healed," Tom explained. "I no longer had difficulty breathing and did not cough at all."

Even so, his wife insisted that he make an appointment to see his doctor.

"I will never forget the look on my doctor's face as he listened to my lungs," Tom said.

The doctor asked, "What have you been doing? Your lungs sound perfect."

"I've had people praying for me," Tom replied. "I believe God healed me by performing a miracle."

The doctor agreed that there appeared to be no other explanation.

"God knew that in my heart I wished to be healed and wanted to see my children grow into mature adults. I wished very much to live to support them and my wife. But God knew that my faith in Him did not depend on receiving a miracle," Tom has said.

Years ago we moved to another state but keep in touch with our friends. Tom is now eighty-two years old. I recently telephoned Tom and Lorraine, and both confirmed what I had remembered about the healing. Tom returned to his normal work until he retired. He had no idea why he was chosen to be healed or why it happened shortly after he attended the healing service, but both he and his wife believed attending the service was related to Tom's miracle.

At least forty-five years have now passed. The emphysema never returned, nor have any of the symptoms.

As Tom so desired, he has enjoyed life with his wife by his side and watched his family grow to adulthood. His message throughout the years remains the same: "I trusted the Lord's decision, and He chose to heal me by His amazing power."

The miracle changed Tom's life and touched many others. The miracle reinforced his faith that God heals who and when He desires. Tom and Lorraine's faith remained firm even when his lungs, according to the doctor's prognosis, were "untreatable" and there was no hope of healing.

A few days ago I received the yearly Christmas letter from the Bunners. I was delighted to read, "Today we are healthy." They also wrote, "We are rejoicing in the great love showered on us by God and our family."

I join the Bunners in their thankfulness to God.

The Jesus Hug

JON HOPKINS

I buried my wife, Renee, one week after Valentine's Day. For the next year, I cried every day. On one of those sad days, I could not motivate myself to do anything. I just sat in my brown faux leather recliner. I hated to turn the TV on as I knew I would only channel surf and might run into something that could make me sad. It may just be a cute commercial about a kitten or even the news. It didn't take much to remind me of losing her.

I decided to watch one of those singing competitions I had recorded on TV. It would entertain me and get my mind off of my grief. The singers gave their best live performances before discerning judges. My seventeen-year-old extremely fat orange tabby cat lay lazily on my feet. My other cat—a white stray—slept in a chair. I relaxed and enjoyed the small bit of comfort and rest from grieving.

Before long, a contestant sang a wonderful song that really moved me. I muted the TV.

"That was great!"

The cats didn't respond.

Silence.

My wife and I had always muted commercials so we could talk to each other while watching TV. It was one of our favorite things to do together. But this time, after I called out that I thought the singer was great, only silence responded. I had no one to share that experience.

I was alone.

I looked at a picture of my wife on the table beside my chair. I had put it there to comfort me and to remind me that she was still present, even if in heaven.

"Where are you?" I implored.

I often talked to her picture, or to her empty seat in the car. Sometimes I pretended she was with me when I went to the movies by myself. I always made sure there was an empty seat next to me. I would place my hand on the theater seat hoping to feel a bit of warmth as if she had just gotten up to get a drink and would be right back.

I told the picture that I missed her. I missed her a lot. I told her that since she had died the previous year, I missed her more than I could handle some days. I missed her smile, her laugh, her ideas, and the way she would lick her lips just before we kissed. But what I missed the most was her touch.

"I've cried every day since you died. For a little over a year, I haven't held your hand, touched your face, or felt your loving arms around me when we hugged. I miss your hugs."

At the word *hug* I broke into heaving sobs.

In the middle of my grief quake—followed by a grief tsunami—I looked up and I began to pray.

"Jesus, will you please send me a real hug? I need . . ." I lowered my head to my chest and softly finished, " . . . a real hug."

As my weeping subsided, I turned the TV sound back on. My white cat jumped into my lap and purred. I numbly finished watching the show.

Later that day, I got ready and went to work. I worked three evenings a week at a Christian bookstore. Getting busy in my daily routine, I forgot all about my prayer. I just kept moving like I always did just to get to the next thing.

The bookstore was a sanctuary for me. It had a coffee shop on one side, and I always felt I got paid in delicious free coffee aromas when I went to work. Some nights the bookstore was quiet. Some evenings it was busy with foot traffic. The coffee shop seemed to always have some people in it. They talked and laughed; they studied for classes at school. But the bookstore was not always so busy.

That night it was slow. There were few customers, and they were far between. After four hours of standing at the cash register, straightening books, and dusting shelves, I was pretty bored. I tried to keep my mind busy.

At nine-thirty a young college couple came into the shop. They had been in before. Some days I liked watching them as they held hands and laughed together while browsing through the books. He wore a Kansas Jayhawk shirt and had a gregarious smile. Her chestnut brown hair—straight and long—flowed softly over her shoulders and down her back.

He touched her side and she giggled. They were obviously in young love. But tonight it began to bother me. I felt another grief-burst well up as though I were a pop can that had been shaken up too long. The remembrance of touch was tugging on the aluminum pull tab.

I quickly turned and focused on alphabetizing a shelf of cookbooks near the checkout counter.

Soon the young man and woman came to the cash register. He wanted to buy his girlfriend a ring. It was nothing expensive; it was simple, silver, and delicate. He leaned across the counter and said, "Don't let her see how much it costs."

She protested. They argued playfully as I rang up the sale.

Then, while the man signed the credit receipt, I couldn't contain my thoughts on their little lover's quarrel any longer.

"If you don't mind my telling you something," I said. His look told me that he could tell I was serious. She placed a hand under his arm. "Don't ever neglect the opportunity to get something for the one you love." Then I looked straight at her. "And don't ever worry about the cost." I looked down while putting their purchase into a sack. "And do it often." Then softly, "You don't ever want to look back and say, 'I wish I could've loved her more.'"

Perhaps the girl heard something in my voice. In the pause of handing them their purchase, she asked the one question I really didn't want to answer, "Why do you say that?"

It all came out. I told them about my wife's passing. I told them how it was a sudden and unexpected heart attack.

"We'd been married for thirty years." I went on and on and told it like I had rehearsed it so many times. I'm sure I said more than I remember. Like the proverbial opened pop can, I spewed my grief.

When I finished, they were silent. Not unlike the quiet muting of the TV earlier that day. The girl looked at me. With tears in her eyes she asked, "Do you mind if I give you a hug?"

She didn't wait for my answer. She stepped around the counter.

As she reached out to me, I held up my hands and stopped her. Sudden realization flooded my heart. My resolve broke and I sobbed openly in front of her.

"I—I—I—I prayed this morning for—for t-t-this. I prayed for—a real hug."

She grabbed my shoulders. Then she pulled me in very close. Enfolding me in her arms, she put her cheek against my tear-stained chin. She hung on . . . and on.

I relaxed into her hug and I cried.

I whispered, "Thank you."

"No, thank you," she whispered back.

In my heart I said thank-you to Jesus.

We talked awhile more. The young man said something about that ring gaining more importance because of our talk. We said several good-byes. And I was left alone again. Only it was a different alone: one where I didn't feel alone. Jesus had given me a hug.

Later that night, when I got home, I posted this status on my Facebook page: "Today, in my loneliness, I prayed for a real hug. . . . And God sent me one! He meets our every need!"

I got several responses and "likes." And then I received this comment:

"Guaranteed way to get hugs is to give them!"

I am sure that this person meant encouragement to me by that remark. It was someone whom I really trust and gain strength from. And I appreciated the comment. I didn't want to leave Jesus out of the equation, though.

I responded this way on my page:

"Well, I could give hugs to random strangers all day, I'm sure. But there is a big difference when someone unsolicited initiates a hug at just the right time you need it to show they care. My hugging someone may get me what I want, but it does not meet that deep-felt need and longing for connection and touch I desired . . . and received. Therefore I say it was of God . . . and not of me."

I hoped my friend realized there was a difference. God truly answered my prayer. He sent Jesus in the person of a young girl with real arms to give me a real hug when I needed one, and it touched me in a very special way.

When a Door Closes, Keep Knocking

ANN ELIZABETH ROBERTSON

Another baby shower!"
I winced.
"I have nursery duty?"
I balked.

Too many church events prodded that inner aching to surface and deepen.

I finally confessed to my husband, Doug, "Lately, I've been hurting for a baby. Why?"

From others' perspective, we had a perfect family of three: a father who was secure in his family business, a mother who taught in the Christian school during the week and children's church and Sunday school most weekends, and a beautiful nine-year-old daughter who was full of personality and life.

While all around me others were growing their families, I had been content, knowing I couldn't have more children. A cancer scare when I was twenty-seven, and the unavoidable hysterectomy, had closed that door. Only now I wanted to be a mother of two, a mother who held her own baby during nursery duty.

So were there other doors to knock on?

My asking, seeking, and knocking began the afternoon my friend Sarita asked, "Would you ever consider adopting? We know someone in Memphis whose daughter just gave birth to a baby boy; they realize the baby should go to a family who wants him."

Lord Jesus, please guide us. Is this our baby?

Doug and I quickly hired an attorney who began working out the details for this private adoption. I prayed 24/7, or so it seemed. Two weeks of filling out paperwork, and we were hours from meeting Matthew Scott, our new son.

Then our attorney called. "She's changed her mind."

I cried all afternoon.

Back then there were no Internet searches—just libraries, lots of letter writing, and word of mouth. My daily prayer became, "Guide us, Lord Jesus. You know where our baby is."

Throughout those two years, amid the great disappointments of "almost" babies, I grew to trust the all-wise God. He knew who each baby's mother should be. Maybe my prayers of intercession had helped these birth mothers decide to keep their children. Maybe I'd have to wait for our Isaac and not mistakenly coerce an Ishmael into our home.

And with each closed door, I repeated Matthew 19:26, "With God all things are possible."

Those were my faith-breathing days, often countered with smothering days of doubt. Like a memorable chapel time at the school where I taught. I was feeling low and simply bowed my head and prayed, "Am I bothering you, Lord, with my constant prayers for a baby?"

Within minutes the minister shared his message from Luke 18. "There was a widow who persistently pleaded her case before the judge. Verse one reads: 'Then Jesus told his disciples a parable to show them that they should always pray and not give up.'"

Got it, Lord!

But just in case I didn't, the following Sunday another minister spoke from Matthew 7:7–8: "Ask and it will be given to you; seek and you will find; knock and the door will be opened to you. For everyone who asks receives; the one who seeks finds; and to the one who knocks, the door will be opened."

Hope filled me—that is, for another few months. Then one still-dark morning during my prayer time, I pleaded, "If we can't have a baby, could you please help me stop wanting one? What is your plan?"

Kneeling next to the recliner, I flipped my Bible open to Psalm 66. Hmm, God made a way for the Israelites. *So couldn't He make a way for us?* He refined and purified them as silver. *Is that what this is?* He brought them through fire and water into a place of abundance.

Then David's words read, "If I regard iniquity in my heart, the Lord will not hear me; but certainly God has heard me; He has given heed to the voice of my prayer. Blessed be God, Who has not rejected my prayer" (vv. 18–20 AMP).

With that last phrase I heard a "yes!"

I reread each line, especially about "iniquity in my heart."

Okay. It's not so hard to rid my heart of iniquity, a lot like a daily scrubbing. No, it was the refining, purifying, fire, and water that got tough.

Frozen days followed—iced-in days of an endless winter. A week of school was cancelled, and I arose early each morning, praying with authority, "In the name of Jesus, let the telephone ring with word of our baby."

Hopeless silence stilled the air.

During those drawn-out days, I chose to relinquish my impatience. I decided to develop a deeper trust in God's timing and to build a faith that was sure of what I hoped for, even with no evidence in sight.

Through a turn of events many might call coincidences, a man named Daniel walked across our path, visiting our church as a guest speaker.

"I'd like to pray for all the young couples today," he announced at the end of the service. A long line formed, with Doug and me at the end of it. An hour passed, and Doug's stomach was growling for lunch.

"We can't leave now," I whispered as I heard couples before us asking for prayers for healing in their relationships and finances.

"Any needs?" Daniel asked when we got to the front of the line.

"Well, our lives seem so good right now," I started saying, feeling guilty that I was taking his time. "Except that we'd love to adopt a baby. . . ."

Daniel's face brightened. "I was just at a fund-raiser last weekend for a new adoption agency. Let me get you the address."

And thanks to divine appointments, I contacted a ministry birthed out of a megachurch to provide support for pregnant teenagers. All my contacts were kind and informative, and just as I'd done with the previous agencies, I filled out mounds of forms.

Joan, one of the agency's administrators, cautioned us, "It might be years. You won't know anything until after the baby is born and the birth mother has had time to decide. We don't assign babies to the next couple in line. Our council prays for the right family and where each baby belongs."

In the following months my faith was in the unseen. Yet my human preference was to see something tangible. So for my own inspiration I set up a visual of what I was hoping for—I put up a beautiful watercolor painting of an infant boy's face, loosely wrapped in a swirl of white and blue blankets. Underneath it I wrote 1 Samuel 1:27–28: "I prayed for this child, and the Lord has granted me what I asked of him. So now I give him to the Lord. For his whole life he will be given over to the Lord."

Call me a persistent widow and an annoying door-knocking neighbor, but each day I learned how to hear God's voice, trust in Jesus' words, and be guided by the Holy Spirit. I made bold changes, like in May when Doug and I agreed I shouldn't teach school the following year, just in case. I asked Jesus to somehow not only let me know when our baby boy was born, but to let me take part in the baby's birth somehow, either physically or spiritually.

And our busy lives carried on. All the while that prayer for Matthew Scott swirled around us, a part of who we were becoming: parents of our new baby with our daughter, Ari, becoming a sister.

As August approached, I directed a children's play at church. Innumerable details consumed those months, but thoughts of Matthew were still intertwined in my focus.

Then another memorable moment came one afternoon while I was driving to a friend's to consult with her about the costumes for the play. While I sped down a back stretch of road, I heard the thunderous words: "You will have a nine-pound, ten-ounce baby boy, twenty-one inches long."

When I reached Debby's house, I stumbled through her door, telling her about those bold, clear words.

"What does it mean?" I asked.

"I'm not sure," Debby said. She laughed. "Let's hope that isn't his birth weight!"

That evening I described my experience to Doug, once more reminded of the past two years, the Scriptures, the dreams. Yet no phone rang, no door opened.

With the children's program behind me, I finally had my first quiet Friday in October. Or I thought I'd have a quiet Friday. Until lightning pain struck my abdomen, forcing me to bend over. Again it hit. Finally I called Doug.

"It feels like I'm in labor," I explained, forcing myself into bed. *Could it be? Hadn't I asked the Lord to let me be a part?*

Saturday, I was still weak. Sunday, I pushed to go to church and to a family outing. As I walked down the aisles of the craft fair with Doug and Ari, my labor-like pain returned with greater intensity.

"I have to go home," I finally said.

Another week passed with no phone call. That Tuesday, after dropping Ari off for school, I arrived at the office where I did volunteer work. On my desk I found a savings passbook my mother-in-law had dropped off the day before.

The note read: "This account was opened eight years ago. We don't want you to pay us back. It's yours. Love, Mimi."

I called the bank, and with the interest compounded, the account had $814. What a great surprise. Even though Doug and I had set aside the exact amount the adoption agency required for a possible adoption, our monthly budget was tight.

The day only got better, though, with our greatest surprise that afternoon when the phone rang. Don, the administrator of the adoption agency, announced, "A nine-pound, three-ounce, twenty-one inch baby boy has been born. We've prayed and believe this is your baby!"

I shouted.

Doug, who was on the extension phone, said, "But Ann, didn't you say nine pounds, ten ounces?"

"So I heard wrong and missed it by seven ounces," I countered.

"Hang on just a minute," Don said. I heard him shuffle papers. "Let's see, the baby had a checkup this morning. His weight as of today is nine pounds and ten ounces. Does that mean something to you?"

"Yes!" And once I explained, Doug and I compared notes with Don.

Unbelievably, our birth mother had gone into the hospital with complications the Friday I had "labor pains." She had given birth to Matthew on Sunday afternoon while I unknowingly labored with her. Jesus had honored my request that He not only let me know when our baby was born but allow me to take part in the process somehow.

"There's one problem," Don interjected. "Her complications added eight hundred dollars to the amount we told you it would be last year."

"Not a problem," I confirmed.

I will always love Matthew's birth mother. One of the sweetest answers to my prayers was that this pregnancy brought salvation to her and her parents. As a young teenager, she lived with one of the church family members, accepted Jesus, and provided Matthew a safe and loving environment within her womb.

God had me in His womb, too, nourishing me, growing me. In hindsight, had we been able to adopt Matthew easily, my faith would have never deepened with such dimension, wider and longer and stronger. It took the silent times, the aching hours for me to know without a doubt that God was with me even when I didn't *feel* His presence.

All that asking, seeking, and knocking was not in vain. Our Lord Jesus had taken care of it all, and He opened the door wide for us to welcome our son, Matthew Scott.

Friend of the Fatherless

·•·————·•·

ARIA DUNHAM

On the edge of the ocean in Key Biscayne, I sat with my two boys, ages six and seven. The breeze was mild, the heat high, and the sky filled with night stars. A full moon cascaded glistening light along the water's waves like a blanket.

On this Father's Day we were three fatherless children. The legacy of a broken home had been passed down to my children.

For years my father had abused me, and after forgiveness and confrontation, I had to cut ties to keep my sanity. And now my children were facing the same kind of estrangement from their father. For months he hadn't called or visited, and divorce changed an intact family home into living in two separate states and lives that rarely intersected.

"Give thanks to all the dads here today! If you're a dad, please stand up so we can acknowledge all your hard work and dedication," the preacher had said in church that morning. Dads stood up next to wives and children.

My boys looked around the sanctuary, seeing all the fathers and knowing no one stood next to them. My eldest leaned in to my arm and nestled a head to my side. The other sat stone-faced, eyes and mouth hard and emotionless. Next to each son was a craft with a photograph that said, "Happy Father's Day, Dad," decorated with half-torn stickers and scribbles.

But their dad wasn't here, and they didn't have anyone to give that picture to. There was no man to claim these gifts of loving labor.

We went home. The day felt longer than any Sunday ever before.

"Lord, what do I do with these kids?" my heart cried. "Look at them. They are hurting like you know I hurt. No one wants to be a dad to them. No stranger ever accepts orphans unless they are from some distant village. How many times, Lord, did I look for a dad, anyone's dad, to be there for me? I don't want them to search like I did only to be convinced that no one would ever be there. I am heartbroken."

The voice broke my cry. "Wasn't I always there beside you? Aren't I Yeshua, the One who made you? Didn't I claim you? Am I not Father? Cast your cares on me."

Stunned and speechless, I remembered small miracles . . . where evidence of Jesus' protection was displayed in my life.

Was the heartbreak these two little ones felt any different? It was death knocking at their lives to rob, kill, and destroy hope and hide identity.

And He was there, Jesus, my pathway to my heavenly Father . . . theirs . . . mine . . . ours, one God of all generations, mine included. The legacy of brokenness, gone. Where could we go to feel Jesus closer than here?

"Grab your sandals," I told my children as they sat on the sofa watching television.

One child's trance broke and his gaze turned to me. "Where are we going?"

"To spend Father's Day with Jesus. Where He called out His followers. The place it all began," I answered.

One hour later we arrived at the ocean. The three of us sat, sandy bottoms, paper, pencils, matches, on Key Biscayne sand. The sounds of waves rolling cried out to my heart, *Yeshua. Yesh-u-ahh.*

Their eyes traced the line of the water's edge as the sun's fire sank beneath the coolness of a wet horizon.

"Here," I handed each child a blank sheet of paper. "Take this and write *Happy Father's Day* on it."

"Why?" my oldest asked. "No one is here but us."

"Trust me," I assured him. "It'll all make sense."

They scribbled. I scribed. Three of us wrote each word in large letters. When we were finished I said, "Next, write what you wish your dad would do for you but hasn't. If he made you sad or mad, write that word under what you wanted but didn't get from him."

One wrote, "Play with me."

The other wrote, "Watch TV."

I wrote, "Say you're sorry. Love me."

When each of us finished writing, I said, "Now tear the paper up in tiny pieces. We are going to burn them and put the ashes into the water."

Puzzled faces stared at me.

"Why, Mommy?" The oldest son asked, scrunching up his nose.

"Do you remember the story when Jesus called out to the fishermen and they became part of His family? That happened at a beach. This is where it all begins, again. Jesus said for us to cast our cares on Him."

Small smiles formed on their faces. Eyes shined in the moonlight. Hands tore paper. We piled the broken pieces on dirt and rocks in the middle of the circle where we sat.

"He is here. This is a new beginning for us. Let's ask Jesus to take these hurts and make them better. I think He hears us. He made us. He loves us. He and His Father."

Holding their hands, I prayed out loud, "Father God, we know you love us, that you made us, that we are your children. Take these broken pieces and remember us. We love you. Happy Father's Day. In Jesus' name, amen."

Then I lit a match. We watched the flame burn each small piece until the last flicker of light was gone.

"Okay, grab a handful of the ashes and put it in the water," I instructed them. "And remember that no matter what, you have a Father in heaven. . . . No matter what happens—whether it gets better or worse—Jesus is always with us."

Then the three of us, a human trinity before the Holy Trinity of all creation, stood beside the edge of the ocean . . . the face of the void of the deep. With ashes, dirt, and stone in our hands, we cast our cares on Jesus, like invisible nets. Believing He will hear, and asking, *Catch us, Jesus, like fish.*

Precious Promises
Come True

JANE OWEN

I grasped my husband's hand and pressed my back against the padded chair across from the doctor's walnut desk. Trying to breathe normally, I wondered, *What will my fertility tests show? Lord, I want to be able to have a child.*

My heart quickened as the door opened. Dr. Bauer entered, shuffling papers in my patient folder.

"Hello, Ron and Jane," he said, extending his hand to us. "I'm sorry to keep you waiting."

He eased into his desk chair, peered over his dark-rimmed glasses, and politely smiled. "I won't parse words with you. . . ."

I braced myself as he continued. "You both are healthy, but," he said, directing his gaze at me, "Jane, your test results indicate the infection you suffered as a child has caused scar tissue to form around your reproductive organs." He pressed his lips together. "They are unable to function properly."

Ron leaned toward Dr. Bauer. "Are you saying we can't have a baby?"

Dr. Bauer shook his head. "It's highly doubtful—I'm sorry," he said, giving us both a professional look that numbed my heart.

He picked up my records and stood. "There is another option," he said, stepping around his desk. He rested his hand on my shoulder. "I want you to go home and consider applying to adopt a child."

"Adoption?" I replied, looking into his brown eyes.

"Many children need families," he said. "You and Ron would be loving adoptive parents."

On the way home, I stared out the window, watching drivers cut in and out of the freeway traffic. *Lord, adopting a child might be wonderful, but . . .*

When we pulled into our driveway, Ron took my hand and gave it a gentle squeeze. "Don't be disappointed, Jane. We've asked the Lord for a child, and I believe He's working out a plan that's just right for us."

I gave him a pasted-on smile, then burst into tears.

"I know that's true, Ron," I sobbed. "Pray that I can accept the Lord's plan for us."

The next couple of months challenged my faith. I forced myself to attend two baby showers and celebrate my friends' anticipation of the arrival of their babies. I cried each time I drove home from those occasions.

I'm trying to trust you, Lord! I knew down deep *trying* and *trusting* didn't go together.

Late one night, a gentle touch on my forehead awakened me. I sat up and noticed that Ron was sound asleep. I started to lie down again when my heart heard, "Make a written record."

Are you speaking to me, Lord?

I slipped out of bed and got on my knees. "What should I write down, Jesus?"

Immediately, Psalm 128 came to mind. Quietly, I left the bedroom and went to our family room.

Sitting in our recliner, I opened my Bible to Psalm 128. My eyes focused on verse 3: "*Your wife will be like a fruitful vine within your house; your children will be like olive shoots around your table.*"

These promises couldn't wait until morning. I went back to the bedroom and shook Ron's shoulder.

"Honey, wake up," I said. "Jesus spoke something to me!"

I turned the light on and handed the open Bible to Ron. "Read Psalm 128, verse 3."

He sat up on the side of the bed and read the entire psalm aloud. Then, with a big smile, he said, "That's a pretty clear word from the Lord." He took my hand. "Let's believe these promises for ourselves, Jane!"

"Wait a minute!" I exclaimed, sitting next to my husband. I pointed to the last verse he had read. "That sixth one says we'll see our children's children!"

Ron prayed, "We trust you to make these verses real for us."

"Yes," I agreed. I hugged my husband and said, "Only Jesus can make the impossible possible."

The next morning was the last day of March, and a light dusting of snow covered everything. My good friend Diana stopped by to visit.

"Guess what Jesus told us last night!" I blurted out as I hung up her coat.

She studied my face and grinned. "Are you pregnant?" she asked.

I laughed.

"Not yet—but soon!" I replied. "I'm expecting to be expecting!"

Diana and I sat in front of the fireplace and enjoyed cups of spiced tea. The crackling fire punctuated our conversation.

"Maybe you'll be pregnant, Jane, before Emil and I get married in May," she said.

I smiled and tapped my cup. "Maybe," I said, staring into the warm fire. Suddenly, I remembered. "Oh, there's something else to tell you!"

"What?" she asked, leaning toward me.

"Last night, before the Lord directed me to Psalm 128, I felt His hand brush my forehead. I thought it was Ron, but I heard these words in my heart: 'Make a written record.'"

Diana and I sat quietly for a moment.

"Do you have a package of greeting cards?" she asked.

"I'm sure I do," I replied, getting a box of cards from a cabinet nearby. "Why?"

She smiled. "I have an idea. You could use it to write down Scripture promises from the Lord," she explained.

I nodded and thumbed through the stack of cards. "How about this one?" I said, holding up a sample. "It says, 'For Your Special Day.'"

"Perfect!" Diana exclaimed.

I grabbed a pen and opened the small card with its simple design of a tree surrounded by flowers. "Listen to this inside greeting," I said. "'May your day be all you hope it will be!'"

Diana took a sip of tea and commented, "You and Ron have been hoping to have a baby for a while now—that makes me think of Hebrews 10:23."

Quickly, I opened my Bible to that verse.

"This is good," I said. "It says when God makes a promise, He keeps it!"

For the next hour, we shared encouraging Scriptures about the promise of children. I listed several on the inside of the "Special Day" card, beginning with Psalm 128:3 and 6. "I can't wait to show this 'written record' to Ron!" I said, adding the twenty-third verse of Hebrews 10.

When Diana left, I continued to thank the Lord. I felt His loving embrace filling me with contentment. As I prepared dinner that evening, I sang, "I do trust you, Lord! You are faithful to me, in every way. Throughout each day, I'm rejoicing in your loving promises that will not fail."

Ron arrived home from work, and after dinner we read the Bible verses I had written in the card earlier that day.

"What about Psalm 127:3?" Ron suggested.

"I'll read it," I said, turning to the verse. "This is beautiful!" I exclaimed. "'Children are a heritage from the Lord, offspring a reward from him.'"

I threw my arms around Ron's neck. "These promise verses are like precious treasures!"

The following months brought no pregnancy. I reread the verses in the card. One particular day, I put my hands on the recorded promises in the card and said, "These are true, Jesus. No matter what I see or feel."

That affirmation was about to be tested.

In July, Diana called with news. "Jane, Emil and I are going to have a baby!"

My heart lurched. Forcing a happy response, I said, "That's wonderful. When are you due?"

I really wanted to hang up the phone. *She just got married and she's pregnant already—but I'm not!*

I called Ron in tears, asking, "Can you come home? I need you."

The moment he came through the door, I screamed, "I'm *angry!*"

He held me, and we sat together on the couch as I told him what had happened. Stroking my face, he whispered, "Jane, I understand, and so does the Lord."

I pushed back from my husband. "I'm beyond mad—I'm jealous!"

Ron began to pray. "Lord, we give you our selfish mistrust right now. . . ."

"I'm sorry, Jesus," I sobbed. "Help me! I want to be happy for my friend, not jealous."

That's when I went to the phone to call Diana.

"Forgive me, Diana," I said. "I was full of envy when you told me your baby news."

"I hesitated to tell you, Jane. I didn't want to hurt you," she added in a sweet tone.

I took a deep breath. "You didn't hurt me. It was the anger that welled up in me that threatened to upset my faith."

That summer of 1978 waned, and nippy air warned of an early fall. I remember thinking, *I'm still expecting to be expecting, Lord. How much longer?*

At midnight on September 16, Ron woke me up. "Jane, the Lord just spoke to me—I heard Him!"

What? Am I dreaming? I threw the covers back and turned to Ron. "Did you say you heard the Lord?"

Ron was quiet for a moment. "This is amazing!" he said. I leaned closer to my husband as he continued. "Jesus told me: 'This night, I have opened your wife's womb. She will conceive and have a son. Name him Aaron Michael for he will be strong in my Word.'"

We held each other as those words spread warmth through

my body. I cried and laughed at the same time. *You are giving us a son! Thank you, Jesus!*

The ending weeks of September signaled no change; but by late October, I noticed some differences in my body. I called Dr. Bauer's office and made an appointment for November 4.

That day, Dr. Bauer's manner was routine when I told him, "I think I'm pregnant."

I noticed the slight frown as he replied, "I know that's your hope, Jane. Sometimes our bodies can mimic pregnancy, but I'll check." He patted my hand.

A few moments later his manner changed. "You are expecting!"

I smiled. "How far along am I?"

"Everything tells me you are seven weeks pregnant," he answered.

I quickly calculated the weeks from September 16. *Seven exactly!*

"Dr. Bauer, I have something to tell you. . . ."

When I finished relating our story, he said, "That is the most wonderful account I can remember hearing." In his excitement, he left the room and announced to his staff, "This patient is pregnant, and I didn't think it was possible!"

Although I encountered some problems the first couple of months, the prayers of faithful friends helped us keep our faith-footing. On June 7, I went into labor about five-thirty in the morning.

I have plenty of time, I thought. *I won't wake Ron yet.*

But in an hour, my contractions were ten minutes apart. I headed to our bedroom to rouse my husband.

By 8:15 I was in the delivery room, concentrating on my Lamaze breathing.

"Dr. Bauer is on his way," a nurse said in a measured tone. "You shouldn't have to wait much longer."

Wait? I locked my eyes on Ron's. "Breathe with me, honey," I demanded.

Another nurse bent over me with a big smile. "Your doctor is here now. Are you ready to have your baby?" she asked. I answered with two concentrated pushes.

When Ron and I heard our baby's strong cry, our hearts melted. Then Dr. Bauer announced, "You have a girl—a beautiful baby girl!"

What? A girl?

"Look at your little beauty," Dr. Bauer said, showing us our new daughter. He carefully handed her to Ron, who held her like fragile glassware.

My heart pounded in my ears as I reached for her.

"It's my turn, Papa," I said with a smile.

Gazing at our delicate daughter, I whispered in her ear, "Leah Anne, you are Mommy's perfect surprise."

I turned to Ron. "What a beautiful beginning she is!" I exclaimed. "She proves His promises are bigger than our dreams," I said, kissing my newborn daughter's soft cheek.

Ron and I had thought we were to have only the son God promised us, but when Leah arrived, I realized He planned to give us more children.

My focused hope was for a child. When God surprised us with Leah, that hope grew, knowing our son was yet to come! Yes, God kept His promise and sent Aaron Michael, who was born three years after Leah. Our Lord wasn't finished even then. We later welcomed another daughter, Abigail. God's promises are never one dimensional!

All Things Through Christ

SUSAN E. RAMSDEN

The walls of The Hall were closing in on us. It felt as if all the oxygen had been sucked from the room. My heart raced and my neck muscles tightened. I shifted my weight on the fiberglass chair and sighed, wondering, *How can six girls hijack a couple of professional teachers so easily?*

"Ladies, let's settle down, please," my co-leader, Carol, said, trying to keep her tone pleasant. Her gentle reprimand only exacerbated the problem. The girls shot knowing looks at each other and laughed. One girl who weighed well over two hundred pounds made me uneasy.

"Yes, ma'am," she said with a sinister smirk.

I glanced at the yellow panic button on the far wall.

If we face real trouble, would I be able to reach it in time?

Adrenaline surged through my body, but I tried to appear calm.

On this sultry summer afternoon, Carol and I were beyond discouraged. As we had walked toward the gloomy cinderblock walls, black one-way windows, and razor wire looping the top of the towering fence, she admitted, "Sometimes when I'm driving down here, I hope for a lock-down. I'm so tired of their attitudes. I love them, but some days I just don't want to be here."

This group of incarcerated girls was the most difficult bunch I had encountered in the year I had been going into the juvenile hall to lead a Bible study. They seemed impossible to reach. Sullen and uncommunicative, they seldom responded to or made eye contact with us. On the rare occasion when they smiled, it was in response to the subtle gestures they made to each other across and under the table, gestures that we surmised were gang related.

Sometimes they muttered to each other. When we asked them to share what they'd said, they looked at us with stony faces.

Our morale was sinking fast. It's hard to keep your hopes high when they're met with thinly cloaked hostility. We knew Jesus held the key to their spiritual freedom, peace, and salvation, but they were not interested in our lessons about Him. These teens only cared about being released so that they could return to their boyfriends, life on the streets, alcohol, and drugs. They had no drive to succeed in school, no goals for the future, and no hope of bettering their lives.

This was hard for us to understand, but the most difficult part was that they rejected all of our attempts to teach them about our Lord's unfailing love. We knew Jesus was their only chance for a meaningful, hope-filled future, but they would have none of Him.

Most of these girls had appalling home lives. The majority had never known their real fathers. None had strong role models. Some were victims of incest and other forms of abuse. Some had endured gang rape. Many of their parents were as addicted to drugs and alcohol as they were.

They weren't hardened criminals in the traditional sense; most were incarcerated because they were underage and could not resist the siren song of drugs and alcohol, or were "runners," fleeing from their squalid homes.

Week after week, each Monday afternoon, we shared stories with the girls—tales from *Bad Girls of the Bible*, exploring the lives of real women who had been redeemed by God's gracious love. We hoped the stories would encourage them to trust the Lord and let Him turn their lives around.

But week after week we met the same bored, if not hostile, responses: yawns and glazed eyes that stared past us.

Carol had been volunteering at The Hall for five years when I joined her. She was a seasoned veteran in the war against the enemy. We knew we were fighting powerful spiritual forces that were stronger than either of us, but certainly not stronger than our Lord, who went before and beside us into this forbidding, foreign world.

"Do you feel it, Susan? Do you sense the darkness in here?" she asked.

I assured her that I did. There was a spiritual heaviness in the air.

Some of the girls in The Hall were into Satanism. We could hear their shrieks and thudding on the metal cell doors as they kicked them over and over. Despite our prayers for protection for the girls and for ourselves, I sometimes left The Hall feeling as if I were wearing a suit of lead.

The worst that happened in most groups was that occasionally a girl would express some anger and question the existence of God or His love for her.

We tried our best to help them understand that many of our hardships are results of our or others' free will. Poor choices had caused much of the heartbreak in their lives. We tried to assure them that their suffering wasn't God's fault or His will for their lives. We wanted them to understand that if they would turn their lives over to Jesus, He would redeem the bad times and even bring something good from them.

Some seemed to accept our explanations, but others simply shrugged them off.

But now we had a more aggressive group to contend with, which made our job as volunteers far more difficult. The girls knew we had no real power over them. Carol and I were both retired classroom teachers with years of experience, but nothing had prepared us for the challenges within these prison walls. There was no principal to send difficult girls to for discipline. We couldn't threaten to keep them after school or in at recess.

The most we could do was to send them back to their cells, but my partner seemed reluctant to do that. After all, we were supposed to model Christian kindness, patience, and forgiveness, no matter what.

Finally, after countless interruptions, Carol shut her book and said, "Okay, we're done for today. Time for prayer requests."

She slid six pieces of paper and pens to the girls, who began to write their prayer needs.

Minutes later, as Carol gathered the requests, she noticed a tiny, multi-folded paper on the table. She waved it in the air.

"Does this belong to somebody? Is this a prayer request?"

No one responded.

Again she asked the question but was met with quizzical looks. Shrugging, she tossed it into the prayer box and handed it all to me.

It was my custom to take the prayer box home and copy the requests into an email, which I sent out to the other volunteers so we could pray for the girls throughout the following week. I found the same type of petitions each week for parents, sisters, and brothers, for health, safety, and success in court.

At home as I opened the requests, I silently breathed a prayer for each girl. Some of the appeals touched my heart. One girl asked that God would allow her a furlough so she could attend a niece's baptism. Another asked that God would help her mother and grandmother get off drugs.

These slips of paper revealed the standard prayer requests until I unfolded the *seventh* tiny paper that Carol had questioned the girls about. I sat with my mouth agape as I read: *"I can do all things through Christ who strengthens me"* (Philippians 4:13 NKJV).

I had never seen a note like this in The Hall. The printing did not match any of the girls' handwriting. The ink was a different shade of blue from the pens we used. The paper was a different shape and size. None of the girls were Bible students. They never wrote Bible verses on their papers, nor did they seem to know any. The word *Philippians* was spelled correctly, something I was sure none of these girls could do.

I called Carol and stammered the news of my mysterious find. After a moment she said, "It has to be of the Lord! Where else could it have come from? The table was empty when we arrived. The girls couldn't have written it. What other explanation is there?"

I agreed. I believe Jesus saw our frustration and desperation and knew we needed encouragement to continue to do His work.

How grateful I am that we worship a God who sees us in our struggles, knows our frailties, and cares so deeply about us that He would reach down to deliver a note straight from His heart to ours.

Ever since then, when we are troubled and feel we are too weak to carry on this difficult work of bringing hope to these young, broken lives, we remember that tiny "grace" note and know that truly we can "do all things through Christ who strengthens" us.

His Presence in My Cocoon

CAROL T. SAUCEDA

"Enter into His presence," my counselor told me in response to my desperate plea for help. I was out of answers, tormented beyond my ability to sustain such tremendous pain. I could not feel the presence of the Lord, even though I knew from the Scriptures that Jesus has promised to never leave me or forsake me (Joshua 1:5). Still, I felt as if Jesus had abandoned me or was completely unaware of my anguish of heart. I was in a state of utter despair when I called my counselor for help. But I was beyond her help, wailing on the inside from the grief, disappointment, rejection, and emptiness that I felt.

I had gone to visit my older son, Salvador. I made the trip from Monument to Fort Collins, Colorado, in my 1984 Jeep Renegade. The Jeep was in constant need of repair. I hoped and prayed the Jeep would make the trip. I longed to see my son. I missed him deeply. My younger son, Alan, committed suicide in March of 2000, and Sal was my only child now and all that I had left of my family. I needed to go to him for love and comfort.

The world of my life spun off its axis when Alan died. I experienced absolute, all-encompassing devastation. The wind of life was knocked out of me and did not return. I was suddenly faced with a living death. I was in the throes of horrific pain, sorrow, and grief. I experienced an incomprehensible degree of suffering. The vibrant colors of my life suddenly drained away, turning into just so many shades of gray.

I felt so very alone in my grief. I desperately needed to maintain a connection with Salvador. Alan was gone forever. My marriage had ended. Sal was the last vestige of what my family had been. But we had not been getting along very well before he left home and moved to Fort Collins. He criticized me daily for the medications that I took for the depression, PTSD, and anxiety. He would constantly ask me, "Mom, when are you going to get off all these meds? If you only had enough faith, God would heal you and you wouldn't need to be on all this medication. Mom, where is your faith?" I heard his heart and expression of deep concern for me, but this knowledge could not mitigate the acute feeling of rejection at his scathing words.

Sal did ask me a good question, though. Where was my faith—my faith in Jesus? In truth, my faith was in the midst of a crisis. I asked God, "Why, why, why, did Alan have to die?" I screamed these words at God, terribly painful expressions from the depths of my wounded soul. I was left with no recourse, no way to reverse the death of my son. I had asked a question for which there came no answer from God. However, I remembered what the Lord told me two weeks after Alan's death: "I have prepared you. I have taught your heart to trust my heart and

I have shown you my unfailing love." I pondered the meaning of these words for years.

I still did not understand why Alan died, but I did trust in God's love for me and for my son. I knew that no matter what, no matter how I felt, no matter the overwhelming hopelessness and despair, that I could, and I did, trust God's heart. My faith had become one statement: "Jesus, I trust in thee." I continued to believe that what had happened to my son was somehow a part of God's plan to save Alan unto himself for all eternity. I knew that when Alan died, Jesus was right there as his lifeless body fell to the ground. Jesus received Alan's spirit gracefully into His tender and loving arms. He had shown me this in a vision. The Lord was gracious and merciful to me. He gave me the assurance that I needed to know beyond any doubt that Alan was with Jesus in heaven. My faith did remain intact.

I had seen Sal before I made that frantic phone call to my counselor, and the encounter was not what I had hoped and expected. Before we could even order our drinks at the restaurant, Sal began to criticize me again, in public, for all the medications that I was taking. He pleaded with me out of his own desperation and pain, "I just want my mom back." I was confident in my response. I could only reply, "That person is gone and she is not coming back."

Sal would not accept this and began to argue with me. I knew this was not why I had come to Fort Collins. I could not sustain the complete lack of emotional support. I felt as if a chasm had opened up between us and that I was losing Sal. My already desolated heart could not sustain another loss. I could not bear it any longer. I stood up from the table and said to Sal, "This was a mistake."

I left the restaurant and never looked back. I cried all the way to my Jeep and all the way toward home. The tears would not stop flowing as I reflected on what had just taken place. Before I could get home, I finally had to stop driving and pull off the road. I was beside myself with sorrow upon sorrow. I knew the promise that God would comfort me as a mother comforts her child (Isaiah 66:13), but there is a level of pain for which even Jesus cannot provide relief . . . or so I believed. I would have ended my life then and there if I had the means. That's when I decided to call my counselor.

I told her what happened with Sal and that I was suicidal. I did not know what to do as I was so overcome with agonizing emotional distress. I felt like I had lost another child, a loss that I could not sustain. I described my torment as being in a cocoon, bound so tightly that I could not breathe, just waiting for the spider to come and drain my life away. It was a dark place, void of hope, a very dark place emotionally and spiritually. The pieces of my broken heart were shattered once again. I knew the truth of Scripture that says Jesus came to heal the brokenhearted (Psalm 147:3), but I took no comfort in this knowledge. There was no relief from the onslaught of unmitigated pain. I told my counselor that I did not know how to enter Jesus' presence. She was unable to respond to me in that moment. Then it occurred to me, by the grace of the Holy Spirit, that I might not be able to go to Jesus, but He could come to me.

With this thought and inspiration, I replied to my counselor that I could invite Jesus to come into that cocoon with me, to the place where I was, bound up with the darkness of my soul. Jesus responded immediately to my appeal to His love and mercy. When Jesus entered that cocoon of desolation, I experienced His saving presence. I was instantaneously released from my pain. I knew a solace that I could never have known otherwise. This respite for my soul and spirit also brought physical relief to my body. I stopped crying immediately. A flood of joy and happiness returned to me in that instant. God's promise to comfort me was true and had been applied to my life when I needed it most. He is the Comforter and was able to reach me in a place and time that no one else could.

This swift cascade of peace and comfort could only have come from Jesus. There is no other explanation except for His very presence that delivered me from the black shadows of my soul. Jesus filled me with joy in His presence, just as Psalm 16:11 assures me. My counselor did not talk me into this sudden, astonishing, and wonderful state of being. I had not taken any medications for anxiety or to put me into a temporary pain-killing stupor. The sun did not come out and shine its light on me to cheer me up. The Son came into my life and transformed me, bringing me the relief and consolation that I so urgently needed. I felt not only His presence, but His peace, and most of all His love. I basked in Jesus the Son and felt the penetrating warmth of His great love in my suffering soul.

The love of Jesus continues to sustain me today and forever-more. Jesus' promise has held on to me: "The Lord is close to the brokenhearted and saves those who are crushed in spirit" (Psalm 34:18). Indeed, Jesus has saved me by His presence and shown me His unfailing love.

Too Old to Love Again?

YVONNE KAYS

I t's been six years since my husband died. I am thinking about dating again and some friends suggested eHarmony. What do you think?" I asked my two co-workers on our daily noon walk.

"Well, at your age you certainly can't go looking to meet someone in a bar," my young friend Katie said.

I stifled the laughter that threatened to erupt. I didn't drink, so that was the last place I'd be looking. Still, I cringed at the mention of age.

Maybe fifty-nine is too old to find love again.

But she continued, "After my uncle died, my aunt was lonely. She met someone through eHarmony and now they are happily married. I think you should give it a try. What do you have to lose?"

Hmm—what do I have to lose?

Later that evening at home I tentatively clicked on eHarmony. Using research-based dimensions of compatibility, they promised only matches that held real potential.

Warily I filled out the personal questionnaire. First, a barrage of questions created a personal profile of my interests, values, beliefs, and passions. Then I sorted through fifty things that "I can't stand" and "I must have" in a relationship.

Exhausted as I finally finished, I read, "Congratulations! Shall we send you a match?"

I quickly clicked "No, later please."

Several days passed before I mustered enough courage to click "Yes."

Suddenly I had ten matches to consider from Florida to Arizona. Long-distance romance seemed too daunting; I quickly narrowed my search to the local area. Trying to post a picture was another ordeal. Technologically challenged, I finally mailed eHarmony a current photo to post.

Little did I know that a man I was soon to meet was having the same struggle, urged to seek companionship through eHarmony by his daughter and son-in-law. Fourteen years after a painful divorce he didn't choose, Keith told God, "You have to pick someone for me if it's meant to be. Please let it be the first one I meet."

I responded to a few matches tentatively. Reading Keith's profile, I glimpsed a gentle, kind person who also had strong spiritual values. Using their structured questions first, we began emailing almost every day. I was committed to responding honestly, regardless of what I thought he might want to hear.

"What are you most afraid of in a relationship?" he emailed.

"Not being accepted for who I am," I replied.

"What are you looking for on eHarmony?" he asked.

"Friendship, unless God makes it clear it is to be more," I typed back.

Three weeks later we had our first date. We went to the movies to see *The Chronicles of Narnia* and then spent two hours talking over coffee at Starbucks. Sunday we attended church together, and I discovered his wonderful baritone voice. His hand felt strong and secure as he took mine during prayer times.

"Would you like to have lunch at the coast?" he asked outside the church.

"Great!" I said.

Taking the back roads through the towering Oregon firs, we had a beautiful drive to Pacific City. After lunch he asked if I'd like to meet one of his friends and his family. I was immediately enchanted with his teenage daughters and impressed with his lively interaction with them. I was touched by their enthusiastic welcome and loving hugs.

A week later on his birthday, I gave him a card with reflections I had of him: a young cowboy at fourteen earning money to help support his mother and sisters after his dad died; a musician and an artist seeing beauty in the world; a caring psychiatric nurse, reaching out to those who suffer; a loving father and grandfather; a man seeking God's heart for the changes in his life. His eyes held tears after he read the card.

After a dinner date a few days later, we shared our hearts— our hurts and regrets, the deepest wounds in our lives. As he put his arm across my shoulder and gently stroked my arm, I shivered with a joy that tingled through my body, touching sleeping cords of desire.

When I got home, I said out loud to myself for the first time, "I think I am falling in love."

Suddenly terrified, I ran upstairs, crawled into bed, covered my head, and sobbed uncontrollably. Change is so exciting and so frightening at the same time.

Maybe fifty-nine isn't too old to love again.

The next Sunday was Palm Sunday. I invited Keith to dinner at my house. As he prayed over our meal, he suddenly said something about God blessing his wife. Startled, I looked up at him.

"I guess I better ask you first. Will you marry me?" he said.

Still wearing my first wedding ring, I took it off, laid it on the table, and said, "Yes, I will."

It was only two weeks from our first date.

The following week we met with our pastor and began planning a June wedding. We reserved the wedding location and started telling family and friends.

Sunday brought a glorious Easter morning, but something triggered fear in Keith.

"We cannot get married," he told me, though he could not share his feelings any further. On Monday he canceled the plans at our wedding location and told his family and friends it was off. I was devastated.

"When someone has been wounded deeply in the past, it's difficult to trust. When things move too fast, they retreat. You need to give him time and space," our pastor said tenderly.

Though I cried, I knew he was right.

Later that night I curled up in my bed and told Jesus, "I'm so confused. Am I wrong about this? Is it your will for us to be together?"

Suddenly in my mind's eye, I saw us dancing.

"What do you do when you step on someone's toes?" the question came.

"Say sorry—and try not to do it again," I answered.

"And who is leading?" came another question.

"He is," I replied.

Then I heard in my heart, "You and Keith have to learn to dance together."

Comfort like a warm blanket settled over me and I fell asleep.

We had no contact for a week, then our hearts sang again as we picked up our communication. Our whirlwind courtship continued. Time together brought deeper understanding and trust.

Suddenly, we received word that his mother was failing. His older sister would fly into Portland from North Carolina in a week, and we would take her to northern California, where their mother lived.

"Let's get married when my sister gets here because she won't be able to come again for a wedding," Keith said. "You can meet Mother as my wife instead of my fiancée."

A week to plan a wedding? You've got to be kidding!

"I'll pray about it," I said.

That night I had an incredible dream. Jesus appeared to me dressed in a simple white robe. He said that He had come to tell me how I was to relate to Keith. He showed me four scenes on a giant screen, something like a wall-sized television.

The dream faded and I awoke, awed and amazed at receiving personal instructions from Jesus himself. I tried to replay the messages in my mind, but I could only remember the last two scenes.

In the third scene I saw myself lying beside Keith, facing his back with my arm across him.

Jesus had said, "You are to be his covering."

In the fourth scene, Keith and I were standing side by side, my right hand clasped in his left hand.

Jesus said, "You are to be his helpmate. You are not to be in front of him pulling or behind him pushing. You are to walk side by side."

Marveling that Jesus would speak to me so directly, I now had no doubt that we were to marry. Early the next morning I called Keith and said, "Yes, let's do it!"

And somehow, amazingly, it all came together. Friends said, "How can I help?" They offered to make bouquets, take pictures, pick up the cakes, decorate a unity candle, bring baskets of rose petals, videotape the ceremony, make a ring pillow, and help with announcements—one even wrote a song for us and recorded it for the wedding.

Sunday was clear and sunny, a perfect day for a wedding. I floated down the aisle on the arm of my younger brother to a smiling groom, the church full of friends and family. My heart overflowed.

We were married in May, two months from our first date. Strange indeed how "God sets the lonely in families" (Psalm 68:6). But Jesus knew our journey was not to be smooth or easy, and I think the dream came to strengthen me for what lay ahead.

I moved into Keith's home after a wonderful Florida honeymoon. Our home was a block from the major train route through downtown and in a neighborhood filled with group homes. Homeless people frequented our street. City traffic noises and train whistles woke me several times a night. As a person who thrived on structure and stability, I was thrown into chaos.

Moving from a quiet rural home that I loved and separating from family keepsakes brought a new, deeper level of grief. Blending two households was difficult. We did not need three couches; I gave mine away. Everything was in a new place, and new routines needed to replace old, established patterns.

During seventeen years of living in my peaceful country home, I had never moved the furniture even once. My new husband moved the living room furniture twice in the first month.

Suddenly, I couldn't sleep. I felt lost. I began waking up around three o'clock in the morning, thoughts of items needing sorting or pressures of work looming in my mind. I tossed and turned, feeling inadequate in all areas of my life. I couldn't think clearly or make decisions; I cried for no reason.

Waves of anxiety threatened to paralyze and engulf me. I prayed, family and friends prayed, and my pastor prayed for me. Despite my best intentions and efforts, I floundered in a sea of churning emotions that I couldn't control. Finally, I went to my doctor for help.

"Even good change can cause overwhelming stress," my doctor told me as she recommended an antidepressant. I took the medication.

I found that the only way through this wilderness of anxiety was to walk one step at a time. Every morning I asked for Jesus' help to get through that day; I read and reread God's promises. When paralyzed with fear or indecision, I would ask that my next step be made clear. I celebrated even small accomplishments and achievements.

Gradually the wild, racing, churning emotions gave way to islands of peacefulness and joy. I continued to take the medication, and after several months I felt a normal sense of self returning.

Difficult days continued as two independent people were being melded together. The crucible of marriage burns off the sharp edges, and the process can be painful when communication seems impossible and forgiveness the only way. But always knowing that this was indeed the Lord's will made giving up impossible.

"The Lord Almighty has sworn, 'Surely, as I have planned, so it will be, and as I have purposed, so it will happen'" (Isaiah 14:24). Unmistakably, the dream confirmed this was God's plan and I clung to the promise that what He initiates, He will complete.

Today I am off medication and the anxiety has not returned. My life overflows with blessings as I share life with a loving husband. I keep my arm over him, as Jesus showed me, and I walk beside him. We have moved to a quiet country home in the high desert of Central Oregon with glistening Cascade peaks towering above us. Our eight grandchildren bring great delight and joy into our lives.

And . . . we are still learning to dance together!

The Dancing Angel

Cynthia Vander Haar

F our-year-old Sarah awoke from her nap and staggered sleepily down the hallway into the kitchen, where I stood preparing an enchilada casserole for dinner.

"Mommy, I saw an angel," she said as she came into my arms for a hug.

"You saw an angel?" I asked.

I pictured a seven-foot guardian angel, much like the print that hangs on the children's bathroom wall. It depicts a beautiful, winged protector in a heavy, long gown. She floats above two small children as they cross an old bridge that hangs precariously over a deep gorge.

"Yes, I saw an angel," she said as she yawned and rubbed the sleep from her eyes.

"What was the angel doing?" I asked.

"Dancing."

"Was it a big angel?"

"No."

A few quiet moments passed as I continued to hold her in my arms.

"Wow, that's wonderful that God would let you see an angel in your room."

"And she was dancing," she repeated.

Then Sarah slipped out of my arms and asked for some apple juice. She really didn't have more to say.

But I never forgot.

In kindergarten, Sarah took a beginning dance class after school. She dressed completely in pink for her first recital—pink tights, lacy short dress, hair ribbons, and ballet slippers. Her dad joked that she looked like a little bottle of Pepto-Bismol.

Despite the dance class, gymnastics actually captured her attention for the next five years. She excelled and was soon working her way up the competition ladder and then on to acrobatic gymnastics by the time she was ten. She was always upside-down at the top of a pyramid of young acrobats and loved it.

At that time, my friend Linda and I taught the junior high group at our church. We met once a week to pray for the students. One morning as we prayed, Linda felt like we should stop and pray for Sarah. Even though Sarah wasn't old enough to be in the junior high group, we often prayed for our own children, as well.

I'll never forget that Thursday morning. As we prayed, Linda told me, "I know this is odd, but I feel like we need to pray for Sarah's protection. I sense that her Acro teacher is trying to set her up to be molested."

I looked at Linda in disbelief. Linda had never met him or even been to the gym.

"What? Where did this come from?"

"I don't know," said Linda, "I just feel like he's setting her up somehow."

After the initial shock, I thought a little more rationally. *If this really is a warning from God, what do we need to do?*

So Linda and I prayed, and I told my husband about it that evening. Our discussion went in all directions. It wasn't like we could go down to the gym and say, "Hey! God says you are trying to set our daughter up to molest her!"

What do we do with this?

Sarah didn't have gym again until Monday afternoon. This gave us the weekend to pray and consider the situation. We chose not to tell Sarah about Linda's unusual revelation or ask any leading questions. We didn't want to put any imaginations in her head. What if it wasn't even true? We prayed that God would reveal the secret and hidden things and show us what to do in the meantime.

We asked for wisdom, guidance, direction, protection, and intervention. We asked God to put His angels in the gym to protect all the children from any possible harm. We prayed that any violations would be exposed and that any children that may have been harmed would be healed. And we prayed that the teacher would come to know Christ.

By Sunday night, we didn't have any concrete solutions, but we had peace. Surely God wouldn't reveal something like that without also showing us the way out. We waited.

On Monday morning, Sarah came to the breakfast table and abruptly announced, "I want to quit gymnastics and take dance lessons."

My eyes popped open wide. Was she about to tell me something awful about her Acro teacher? Was I about to hear something no mother wants to hear?

I took a deep breath. I didn't want to appear alarmed.

"Why?" I asked. "I thought you loved Acro."

Milk dripped down her chin as she ate her cereal and confirmed, "I really like dance. I want to quit gymnastics and take dance now."

I questioned her about possible motives to make the change— softly probing to see if she might feel uncomfortable with her teacher. But there appeared to be no real issues.

Was this God's way of moving her out of the Acro class? Had He gently pointed her heart toward dance?

"I really want to do dance." She tilted her head and smiled.

I was amazed but seized the moment.

"Of course you can switch to dance!"

I called the gym and dance offices that very morning and made the changes. I went to the store and bought dance leotards and slippers—pink ones. She started that very evening.

My husband and I continued to pray for the possible risky situation at the gym. A few months later, we heard that Sarah's Acro teacher had been arrested for molesting a young girl at his previous teaching job. He was sentenced to two years in prison. We could only stand in awe of what God had done. None of the students at Sarah's gym had been harmed.

But that is not all. Sarah grew up and majored in dance at Arizona State University, where she is now teaching and pursuing her graduate degree. She established her own nonprofit dance corporation, EPIK, where she is artistic co-director.

EPIK Dance Company is one of the resident dance companies at Mesa Arts Center in Arizona; it also has an impactful anti-bullying program for public schools. In addition, Sarah is a leader for the Be Kind People Project, where her dance crews use hip-hop and spoken word to reach troubled youth in distressed schools across the United States.

It appears that Sarah became much like that dancing guardian angel she saw as a little girl—and today children are safe with her.

"[God] is able to do immeasurably more than all we ask or imagine, according to his power that is at work within us" (Ephesians 3:20).

A Big Answer
to a Fervent Prayer

MARY KAY ROY

The excitement of Christmas was over and winter began. Usually January is a time for me to settle down and regroup, but this year was different. I was starting a new Sunday school class for ladies in my church. I spent my days studying, planning, and asking God to enable me in this new challenge. God's Word had been such an important, life-changing factor for me that I wanted to share it with others.

Since class preparation and the shepherding that came with it claimed much of my attention, I was slow to notice a change in my quiet husband's spirit. Discouragement edged his eyes and voice, and he was dissatisfied with his work.

Shane was forty-three, a pediatric nephrologist (kidney disease specialist), an associate professor with the University of Tennessee—Memphis, and head of his section. His work was definitely not boring or monotonous. He taught medical students, residents, and fellows; had a limited private practice; did clinical research; and was co-director of the pediatric dialysis unit.

But all the joy and enthusiasm for his work had disappeared. For weeks I watched him leave for work as tired as a person coming home after a stressful day. He occasionally mentioned problems at work or his discouragement and his feeling of going nowhere.

We did not talk about it often. Talking didn't seem to help or change anything. Because of his personality and dependability, he kept on "keeping on," but with a sense of resignation. Outwardly he looked the same, but I sensed inwardly he felt uneasiness and quiet desperation.

After twenty-three years of marriage I'd become somewhat sensitive to what my husband was feeling. And now he was in such distress that I, too, was suffering. My heart ached for a way to lift his depression. Part of my distress was a sense of helplessness and an inadequacy to alter any of this. There was no way I could meet any of Shane's needs at work.

In May, a friend recommended the book *Men in Midlife Crisis* by Jim Conway. It helped me understand the frustrations and pressures men experience at work, their enormous sense of responsibility to provide for their families, and the daunting realization that they only have a limited number of years to be promoted before society begins looking to younger men.

Understanding these things helped me understand him, but it did not change anything. My main concern became "How can I help this man I have been married to for twenty-three years, this man whose life is so entwined with mine that when he hurts, I hurt?"

I tried to keep domestic problems from being his burden. I made sure our home was a place of refuge and lightheartedness.

But cheerfulness around a depressed person seems to have the opposite effect. I had done everything I knew to do.

Finally, I did what I should have done months earlier. I acknowledged my helplessness and frustration to Jesus. I needed His hand to change things. Many times I've been guilty of telling God how to accomplish the things I pray for. However, this time I only asked Him to do something to restore Shane's joy and enthusiasm in his work.

I am glad I left the details in His hands, for I could never have imagined such a fantastic remedy. "Eye has not seen, nor ear heard, nor have entered into the heart of man the things which God has prepared for those who love Him" (1 Corinthians 2:9 NKJV).

Late in June, God began to move to answer not only my prayer but also the prayers of many parents who were watching their babies starve with an unknown illness.

Two babies with a similar medical puzzle were admitted to the children's hospital where my husband worked. They were not growing, even though they were taking enough formula. Their blood tests suggested an inherited kidney disease.

Although Shane's research is clinical and not done in the laboratory, he has the same inquisitive and searching nature as a laboratory researcher. He and one of his partners began to take steps to solve this malnutrition mystery.

Literature showing the expected ingredients of the formula was checked.

The formula the children were fed was supposed to contain enough of the ingredients necessary for growth. The minerals that were deficient in the babies' blood tests were added to their formula, and they began to respond favorably. That helped to rule out the inherited disease, because the blood tests do not correct that quickly and weight gain is much slower with that treatment.

Then a third baby was admitted with similar symptoms. Shane asked, "What formula is the baby taking?"

"The same as the other two babies" was the reply.

The formula manufacturer was consulted and asked if any similar cases had been reported. No other cases were reported to the company until thirty-six hours after Shane's call. He then had the formula tested by two laboratories, and the mystery was solved. The formula did not contain what its label claimed.

By then the hospital authorities, local health authorities, and the Centers for Disease Control had been alerted. Meetings were held with the manufacturer, various doctors, and health organizations. The formula was recalled from the market. Things were moving fast. Shane was excited. He had been so engrossed in this problem and trying to find the solution that his depression had fallen away. He talked about this event at work, to other doctors across the nation, and at home. The phones wouldn't stop ringing.

God had answered in a way I could never have imagined.

The enormity of this whole thing scared me. Dare I tell Shane of my prayer? If this discovery led to difficulties, would he resent what I had asked God to do?

I watched his enthusiasm and excitement grow as he realized the research possibilities of this experience, and I then felt the freedom to tell him.

One night as we were getting ready for bed, I had just finished brushing my teeth and Shane was eagerly setting the alarm for the morning since he no longer dreaded going to work.

Still holding my toothbrush, I stepped into the bedroom and said, "I need to tell you something."

He looked at me expectantly. After a deep breath I said, "I asked God to do something to restore your joy and enthusiasm for work, but I never dreamed He would answer this big."

Shane fell back on the bed with a sound like he'd been hit in the pit of the stomach. The sudden realization that God had been in control of all this was breathtaking—not the fact that God had done this, but that He had done it for him, and He had done it as an answer to my prayer.

I slept fine that night, having resolved my dilemma of whether or not to tell Shane. But he lay awake a long time, his mind jumbled.

Later he told me his primary thought was to give God the glory for sending this opportunity into his life. He also felt a desire to use this experience to encourage others to pray for their marriage partners and families.

Whenever he has had the occasion to share with others what God has done, he has mentioned James 5:16: "Confess your sins to each other and pray for each other so that you may be healed. The prayer of a righteous person is powerful and effective."

This discovery and subsequent TV coverage led to a representative from our state holding a congressional hearing on recalls and controls on formula composition. This and other hearings culminated in the writing and the passing of the Infant Formula Act, which was signed into law less than a year later by President Carter on September 28, 1980. Shane was privileged to attend the signing of this bill.

This special answer from God brought about the knowledge in Shane's mind that his work was important and that life was not passing him by. His extra effort for his patients paid dividends for many babies across the nation who were diagnosed and treated, and it kept many more from being affected.

This humble man, my husband, who loves and honors God, was honored by God because he persevered at a time when he saw no reason nor had any desire to "keep on keeping on."

Thief Apprehended by Prayer

Bob McCaughan

I had just finished an early evening class in psychology, a class my advisor said I needed to take before starting counseling classes at Denver Seminary. When I returned to the university parking lot, my car was not there; obviously it had been stolen.

Even though I told the security officer that I had already searched the lot and knew exactly where my car had been parked, the man was not convinced. "Look, sir, let's take a ride; maybe we can find your car. Probably right where you left it. A Volkswagen Beetle, blue, right?"

So we drove through every parking lot, looking for my car. *It was a big campus!*

Finally, the security officer offered his opinion. "Looks like your car was stolen. You need to report it to the police and your insurance company."

As if I didn't know that, I thought.

I felt like the officer was still skeptical and viewed me as a scatterbrain. On the other hand, he was kind enough to offer me a ride.

When I got home, my wife, Lillian, and the children wanted to know all the details. After I told them what I knew, we realized it was getting late; it was time for our children to go to bed.

As relatively new and zealous Christians, on the way to seminary no less, we wanted to respond to this situation correctly—in what we felt was God's way. We gathered in our son's room next to his bed for a word from the Bible and prayer. We explained that when people do bad things, God expects us to pray for them. *Bad things*—like stealing our car.

Karen, our twelve-year-old, nodded in agreement. Then Robert said *he* wanted to pray. Five years younger than his big sister, and with a passion and grace beyond his years, Robert prayed earnestly for the thief and the return of our car.

When I reported the theft to the Dayton Police, the officer explained that our situation was similar to others. He cautioned me to be sure of the facts, and make sure that it was a theft—and not something else. He added, "You realize, sir, that your car is over ten years old; furthermore, the locking mechanism on a VW makes it impossible for a thief to steal—unless he has a key."

After several conversations with the police, the FBI, and our insurance company, I realized they were all concerned about possible fraud. The State Police in Ohio had records of several people who had stolen or disposed of their own cars in order to file an insurance claim. Our old Volkswagen fit the profile!

Because of the pervasive cloud of suspicion that hung over us, we prayed all the more. Our seven-year-old son continued to pray fervently for the thief and for him to become a Christian.

Two weeks later the police officer called again. This time, however, his attitude was noticeably different. "We got him! He was driving your car in Indianapolis; twenty-six-year-old guy. You can pick your car up at the police pound in Indianapolis.

"On a different note, Mr. McCaughan, I need to ask you some questions. The man who stole your car just got out of the federal penitentiary in Kentucky. For stealing cars. Apparently, he likes Volkswagen Beetles. Anyway, my question is, Would you consider recommending probation? I realize you're the victim here, but I have to ask, and I need to put your answer in my report."

When the officer asked me that question, I realized that I needed to visit the man first before I could say. So that's what I told him. Then the officer said he had a second question for me.

"Well, Mr. McCaughan, just for the record, since your car was recovered with the key in the ignition, we want to know how he got the key. Did you leave the key in the ignition, or in the car somewhere? Maybe in the glove compartment? Over the visor?"

No! I had not left a key anywhere in my car, so it was a mystery to me how he got a key. Not only was that a mystery, but the car's battery, generator, and electrical system were all nearly dead. So I was amazed that he could somehow start my car and drive it, at night no less, all the way to Indianapolis.

Later that week I arranged to visit the thief in the Dayton city jail. After I got there, the sheriff opened a secure area and escorted me down a long hallway. As we approached the cell area, the deputy hollered, "Victor! You have a visitor."

When I stopped in front of his cell, Victor backed away from the door, apparently alarmed. "Who are you? What you want?" he said as he peered at me from behind the bars.

At that moment, I noticed several things about Victor and his cell. Victor was very short, thin, and young. He probably weighed only about a hundred pounds. The ambience of the cell—the shadowy darkness, the dank smell, and the bare floor and walls—all contributed to a feeling of depression and despair. I was also struck by how lonely and isolated Victor looked. I realized at that moment that I very much wanted him to become a Christian. When I told him that I owned the VW he had stolen, his eyes widened and he again said, "What you want?"

I can only describe what happened during the following hour as something miraculous; somehow, we connected. When I brought up Jesus Christ, and my desire to share with him how Christ had changed my life, he surprised me—he, as it turned out, had a testimony to share with me.

"Sunday night, I was driving your car in Indianapolis on College Avenue. I stopped when I came to the Baptist church. I felt like God was pulling me inside. When I went in, the preacher was talking about Jesus, and he was looking right at me. I knew *God* was talking to *me*. My heart came near to bursting when I went to pray with the pastor. . . . Now, I'm a different man. I want to live for Jesus; I want to tell people about God."

After I got my car back, I found an invoice in the glove compartment. Victor had stopped at a VW dealership; the service department had installed a new ignition switch (with a key, of course), a new battery, and a new generator. So the mystery of the key was solved. And I got my car back in better shape than when it was stolen.

Victor went before a judge, and despite becoming a Christian, he went back to the federal prison in Kentucky. Several months later we received a letter from him; in it he told us a little about prison life. But most important, he had enclosed a chapel bulletin. Victor's name was listed as the Sunday morning preacher!

We lost contact with Victor, but we'll never forget the lesson we learned from the experience: "Love your enemies and pray for those who persecute you, that you may be children of your Father in heaven" (Matthew 5:44–45).

About the Contributors

Connie A. Beckman and her husband, Cliff, live in Helena, Montana, where she works full time and writes from her home. She is an active member of the Cathedral of Saint Helena.

James Stuart Bell is the compiler of this volume and owner of Whitestone Communications, a literary development agency. He is the author or compiler of eight other books for Bethany House Publishers.

Tammy Bowers and Lee Boswell are mother and daughter and live next door to each other in Oregon. Lee's an artist and Tammy's a writer. Both are avid readers who love Jesus.

Guadalupe C. Casillas was born in Nicaragua and now lives in California. She and her husband, Eduardo, have two sons. She is a speaker with Stonecroft Ministries, an evangelistic organization for women.

Julie B. Cosgrove has published several Bible studies, fiction novels, and a devotional collection. Julie lives in Fort Worth, Texas. Visit her website at www.juliebcosgrove.com and her blog *Where Did You Find God Today?* at www.wheredidyoufindgodtoday.com.

Alexine Crawford is a wife, mother, and grandmother. Besides writing, she is a trustee and fund-raiser for charities for disabled people.

Angela Deal lives in Alberta, Canada, with her husband, Dwain. Together, they own and operate a janitorial supplies store. In her spare time, Angela enjoys reading and writing.

Aria Dunham wears many hats, including that of president of the Palm Beach American Christian Writers Association. She lives in South Florida with her husband and their eight children.

Kristi Edington treasures life with all of her family. After going through positive life-changing events, she has devoted her time to sharing God's greatness with all.

Patricia Anne Elford, wife, mother, grandmother, and cat brusher, is an educator, clergyperson, award-winning writer, and editor of shorter pieces and books.

Anita Estes is an art teacher and freelance writer. Her passion is to encourage others in their daily walk with God. She is the author of three books.

Lynnette Goldy is a certified spiritual director, author, and domestic member of the Brothers and Sisters of Charity. She is Greek Orthodox and is married to Eric, an Anglican pastor.

Sandra Merville Hart serves as assistant editor for DevoKids. com and *The Barn Door Book Loft* blog. Her Civil War novella, *A Stranger on My Land*, released recently.

Dennis E. Hensley is a professor at Taylor University and the author of more than fifty books, including *Jesus in the 9 to 5* (AMG Publishers).

Karen R. Hessen lives in Oregon with her husband, Douglas. She has been published in numerous anthologies and devotionals. Karen specializes in nonfiction and humor. Contact her at karenwrites@frontier.com.

Jon Hopkins is married and has two grown children and four grandchildren. He is now a pastor, though his previous roles include psychiatric youth care coordinator, hospital chaplain, church youth pastor, and secondary school teacher.

Yvonne Kays is a member of Oregon Christian Writers and has published short stories and poetry in various publications. She is writing the story of her uncle's experience as a pilot shot down in WWII. Find her at LinkedIn.com.

Maida Keeny and her husband of forty-one years live in Frisco, Texas, where she works from home and spends as much time as possible with her ten grandchildren.

Mary Jo Krump is a freelance writer and editor for Editing Professionals, LLC. She is married with three children and lives in Colorado.

Kristina Landrum was raised in Portland, Oregon, and spent thirty-six years in control of her life. But she says the best years—the last four—"Jesus has been in charge."

Grace Mark has been featured on Todd Friel's radio show and Phil Johnson's popular blog, *Pyromanics*. Grace is completing her narrative nonfiction book, *Fifteen Minutes at a Time*.

Bob McCaughan, now retired, became a pastoral counselor and served at First Baptist Church of Atlanta. He was also employed as the chairperson of the counseling department at Luther Rice Seminary.

Loretta Miller Mehl writes stories about life in the rural South during the Depression. Her work appears in numerous devotional publications. A former secretary in San Marino, California, she now resides in Eugene, Oregon.

David S. Milotta, a retired pastor living in Hawaii, is married and has two adult children. He loves Great Danes, windsurfing, and stand-up paddle surfing.

Jane Owen is a freelance writer whose home is nestled in the mountains of West Virginia. She and her husband have two daughters, a son, and two delightful grandboys.

Janet DeCaster Perrin has served as a women's pastor, Bible college adjunct faculty member, and missions team member. Find her blog at asamaritanwomanspeaks.blogspot.com and www.rainministries.org.

Susan E. Ramsden is a freelance writer, teacher, speaker, wife, mother, and grandmother and has been published in *A Cup of Comfort* series and other publications. She and her husband have coauthored two books.

Ann Elizabeth Robertson retired from teaching secondary English and art to assume her new roles as author, artist, and advocate. See www.annelizabethrobertson.com for more information.

Mary Kay Roy has been a Bible study leader for forty-one years. After her husband of fifty-two years died, she joined a Writer's Circle at church. She has written devotionals for several groups.

Carol T. Sauceda is an author and counselor. She has a heart for those who have suffered great loss and considers it her ministry to help those so afflicted.

Donna Scales is a freelance writer, tutor in the inner-city, skills trainer for the disabled, caregiver for the elderly, short-term missionary, Bible-study leader, women's ministry leader, and prison inmate visitor.

Dana Scott and her husband are chaplains for three separate military organizations: the Oregon State Defense Force, the American Legion, and the Veterans Underage Military Service. They feel honored to be of service to their nation's veterans.

C. F. Sherrow is a retired physician assistant who ministers to other survivors of severe abuse through listening prayer and other scriptural methods. She lives in Colorado.

David Michael Smith hails from Georgetown, Delaware, with his wife, Geralynn; daughter, Rebekah; and son, Matthew. He hopes to be ordained deacon in the Anglican Church. Contact him by email at davidandgeri@hotmail.com.

Evelyn Rhodes Smith is an octogenarian who has been married to Ted R. Smith for sixty-three years. She has been published in various magazines and books.

Connie Sorrell comes from Oklahoma, where she and her husband have raised eight children. Connie publishes essays, devotionals, skits, and puzzles. She has published two books: *Our Family's Darlene* and *A Darlene Summer*.

Cynthia Vander Haar is a mother, grandmother, freelance writer, and a minister for BibleResources.org. She and Daryl, her husband of thirty-nine years, live in Mesa, Arizona.

Susan M. Watkins, award-winning author, wrote for *The 700 Club* and CBN.com. Additional credits include Gloria Gaynor's *We Will Survive* and Max Lucado's website *HisIsMine.com*.

Geni J. White, a retired RN, and her husband of fifty-one years battled her cancer together. He held her hand through every office visit and treatment. They have three adult children.

Jean Ann Williams has published over one hundred articles, stories, and true accounts for various publications. Visit http://joshua-mom.blogspot.com, where she writes about suicide, loss, and hope.

James Stuart Bell is a Christian publishing veteran and the owner of Whitestone Communications, a literary development agency. He is the editor of many story collections, including *Angels, Miracles, and Heavenly Encounters* and *Heaven Touching Earth*, as well as the coauthor of numerous books in the COMPLETE IDIOT'S GUIDE series. He has cover credit on over one hundred books, and he and his wife live in the western suburbs of Chicago.

More Inspiring Stories of God Drawing Near to Us

BETHANYHOUSE

Stay up-to-date on your favorite books and authors with our free e-newsletters. Sign up today at bethanyhouse.com.

Find us on Facebook. facebook.com/BHPnonfiction

Follow us on Twitter. @bethany_house